New England Patriots Trivia Quiz Book

1,100 Questions on Foxboro's Finest

Chris Bradshaw

Front cover image created by headfuzz by grimboid. Check out his great collection of TV, movie and sport-themed posters online at:

https://www.etsy.com/shop/headfuzzbygrimboid

Introduction

Few teams in the NFL can match the achievements of the New England Patriots. That's good for quiz book writers as it gives us plenty of great material to work with.

In the New England Patriots Trivia Quiz Book, you'll find 1,100 questions to test your knowledge on all things Foxboro related.

There are questions covering all aspects of the team's outstanding history, from the early days in the AFL through to the all-conquering teams under Bill Belichick, on to the post-Brady, Mac Jones era.

From quarterbacks to coaches, pass rushers to punters, snowplows to Super Bowls there's plenty here to test your New England knowledge.

The book contains 55 unique quizzes. Each one is made up of 20 questions and centers on a specific theme like rushers or receivers or is a mixed bag made up of a random selection of questions on a variety of topics.

You'll find easy, medium and hard questions so there's something for everyone, from Patriots rookies right up to fans with Belichickian levels of New England expertise.

This compendium contains 500 questions apiece from the New England Patriots Trivia Quiz Book Volumes 1 and 2. All the questions, answers and records have been fully revised and updated so they are accurate to the start of the 2022 season. You'll also find 100 brand new questions which takes the total number of questions up to 1,100.

Now some quick housekeeping. The answers to each quiz are found directly under the following quiz. For example, the Quiz 1 answers are at the end of the Quiz 2 questions. The only exception are the answers to Quiz 55. You'll find these under Quiz 1.

We hope you enjoy the New England Patriots Trivia Quiz Book.

About the Author

Chris Bradshaw has written more than 30 quiz books including titles for Britain's biggest selling daily newspaper, The Sun, and The Times (of London).

In addition to the NFL, he has written extensively on baseball, soccer, cricket, darts and poker for a variety of publications including Bleacher Report, Bluff Europe and The Nightwatchman.

He lives in Birmingham, England and has been following the NFL for over 30 years.

Acknowledgements

Many thanks to Ken and Veronica Bradshaw, Heidi Grant, Steph, James, Ben and Will Roe and Graham Nash.

CONTENTS

Quiz 1: Bill Belichick

1. Whom did Belichick succeed as the head coach of the Patriots?

2. Belichick spent five seasons as the head coach of which AFC team?

3. Before becoming head coach at the Patriots, Belichick spent one day as the head coach of which franchise?

4. Complete Belichick's famous coaching mantra, "Do your…"?

5. What was Belichick's record in his first season as head coach in New England?

6. Belichick was an undergraduate at which college?

7. In what year was Belichick appointed head coach of the Patriots?

8. What is Belichick's middle name?

9. Up to the end of the 2020 season, Belichick had enjoyed more wins as Patriots coach over which franchise than any other?

10. In what city, which is home to an NFL franchise, was Belichick born?

11. True or false – Belichick is older than the Patriots franchise?

12. True or false – Belichick's father Steve was a long-time scout and coach with Air Force?

13. Belichick holds the record for the most successive seasons with at least 10 regular season wins. Which former 49ers coach was the previous holder of that record?

14. In his senior year at college, Belichick was a team captain in which sport?

15. Belichick was just 23 when he started his NFL coaching career after being appointed as an assistant to Ted Marchibroda at which team?

16. Since the AFL/NFL merger, Belichick is one of only two head coaches to have led their team to an unbeaten regular season. Who is the other?

17. The Patriots' first play-off win in the Belichick era was a controversial 16-13 victory over which team?

18. True or false – Belichick made a cameo appearance in the TV drama 'Rescue Me'?

19. Belichick graduated from college with a degree in which subject? a) economics b) physics c) public relations

20. Belichick's first victory as New England head coach was a 28-19 win over which AFC rival? a) Denver Broncos b) Indianapolis Colts c) Oakland Raiders

Quiz 55: Answers

1. Brian Hoyer 2. Mac Jones 3. Stanley Morgan 4. Stephon Gilmore 5. Kliff Kingsbury 6. Nick Folk 7. Stanley Morgan, Irving Fryar, Julian Edelman and Gunner Olszewski 8. Cam Newton 9. Dick LeBeau 10. True 11. Mac Jones 12. Eight 13. Hunter Henry 14. False 15. Second 16. 9 TDs 17. False 18. Cleveland, New Orleans and Baltimore 19. b) 77 20. c) 28

Quiz 2: Pot Luck

1. Long-time New England quarterback Drew Bledsoe played college ball at which school?

2. Offensive lineman Sebastian Vollmer was born in which country?

3. Up to 2022, the Patriots had their worst regular season win percentage of 0.357 against which NFC opponent?

4. What color jerseys did the Patriots wear in Super Bowl LI?

5. Which team has defeated the Patriots in the play-offs more than any other?

6. True or false – Full back James Develin spent his entire college career as a defensive tackle?

7. Between 2007 and 2015 the Patriots used a first-round draft pick on an offensive player only once. Which lineman did they select in 2011?

8. Who holds the franchise record for the most career receiving touchdowns by a Patriots wide receiver?

9. In 2014, Tom Brady sold his California mansion to which hip hop star?

10. Who was the first Patriot to be inducted into the Pro Football Hall of Fame?

11. Which former New England defensive coordinator returned to the team in 2021 as a Senior Football Advisor?

12. Super Bowl LI saw the Patriots make a record-breaking ninth appearance in the big game. Which three teams have appeared in eight Super Bowls?

13. The Patriots won each of their first three Super Bowls by the same margin. How many points saw them home each time?

14. Which Patriots offensive lineman is the nephew of former Broncos, Falcons and Giants head coach Dan Reeves?

15. In which round of the 2009 draft did the Patriots select star wide receiver Julian Edelman?

16. In February 2005 defensive star Tedy Bruschi suffered what serious illness?

17. Tom Brady holds the NFL record for the most play-off appearances. Which receiver's record did he beat?

18. Which special teams ace was the winner of the NFL's Athletes in Action Bart Starr Award in 2017?

19. What is the fewest number of points the Patriots have scored during a full 16-game regular season? a) 181 b) 191 c) 201

20. How many touchdowns did the Patriots score during their record-breaking 2007 regular season? a) 73 b) 74 c) 75

Quiz 1: Answers

1. Pete Carroll 2. Cleveland Browns 3. New York Jets 4. Job 5. 5-11 6. Wesleyan 7. 2000 8. Stephen 9. Buffalo Bills 10. Nashville 11. True 12. False – Belichick Sr coached Navy 13. George Seifert 14. Lacrosse 15. Baltimore Colts 16. Don Shula 17. Oakland Raiders 18. True 19. a) Economics 20. a) Denver Broncos

Quiz 3: 2016 World Champions

1. New England closed the 2016 regular season with how many wins?

2. The Patriots were shut out by which team in week four?

3. The Patriots squeaked past which NFC opponent 23-21 in the season opener after Chandler Catanzaro missed a late 47-yard field goal?

4. In the divisional round play-off, Julian Edelman set the record for the most career postseason receptions by a Patriot. Whose record did he break?

5. Only two Patriots scored a rushing touchdown during the 2016 regular season. LeGarrette Blount was one. Who was the other?

6. Which former North Carolina State lineman started all 16 regular season games plus three play-off games in his rookie season in 2016?

7. How many regular season games did the Patriots win on the road in 2016?

8. Which three Patriot defenders started all 16 regular season games?

9. What was the only NFC team to defeat the Patriots in 2016?

10. With 55 catches and 701 yards, who was the Patriots' most productive tight end in 2016?

11. Only three Patriots had more than 100 yards rushing for the whole of the 2016 regular season. Which three?

12. Who were the five Patriots with over 500 receiving yards during the 2016 regular season?

13. The Patriots signed off the 2016 home regular season with a 41-3 thrashing of which division rival?

14. Who led the team in touchdown receptions in the regular season with seven?

15. True or false – The narrowest margin of victory in a Patriots win in 2016 was one point?

16. Who was the only Patriot named a first team All-Pro in 2016?

17. Which two college programs each provided four players to New England's Super Bowl LI roster?

18. How many interceptions did Tom Brady throw during the whole of the 2016 regular season?

19. How many rushing touchdowns did the Patriots give up in the 2016 regular season? a) 6 b) 7 c) 8

20. The Patriots led the league in scoring defense in 2016. How many points did they give up? a) 230 b) 240 c) 250

Quiz 2: Answers

1. Washington State 2. Germany 3. Carolina 4. White 5. Denver 6. True 7. Nate Solder 8. Stanley Morgan 9. Dr Dre 10. John Hannah 11. Matt Patricia 12. Denver, Pittsburgh and Dallas 13. Three 14. David Andrews 15. Seventh round 16. A stroke 17. Jerry Rice 18. Matthew Slater 19. a) 181 20. c) 75

Quiz 4: Super Bowl LI

1. Which stadium hosted Super Bowl LI?

2. What was the final score?

3. Who was the game's Most Valuable Player?

4. The Patriots overturned a deficit of how many points to claim their historic win?

5. True or false – Super Bowl LI was the first Super Bowl to be decided in overtime?

6. Which former President and First Lady performed the coin toss at Super Bowl LI?

7. Who scored the touchdown in overtime to give the Patriots the win?

8. Who was the oldest player on the New England roster?

9. How many points were scored in the opening quarter of Super Bowl LI?

10. Which Patriot set the record for scoring the most points in a single Super Bowl?

11. How many points did he score?

12. Members of the cast of which hit Broadway musical sang 'America The Beautiful' at Super Bowl LI?

13. Who forced a Matt Ryan fumble in the fourth quarter with the score at 28-12 to give the Patriots renewed hope?

14. Who caught the two-point conversion that tied the game at 28?

15. Only one member of the Super Bowl LI team has a full name that starts and ends with the same letter. Name him.

16. Which five members of the Patriots' Super Bowl LI roster have first names and surnames that start with the same letter?

17. Who was the game's referee?

18. Which singer headlined the half-time show in Super Bowl LI?

19. Who was the only player with 100 receiving yards in Super Bowl LI? a) Danny Amendola b) Julian Edelman c) James White

20. How many yards did Tom Brady throw for during the game? a) 386 b) 426 c) 466

Quiz 3: Answers

1. 14 wins 2. Buffalo 3. Arizona 4. Wes Welker 5. Jacoby Brissett 6. Joe Thuney 7. Eight 8. Malcolm Butler, Devin McCourty and Patrick Chung 9. Seattle 10. Martellus Bennett 11. LeGarrette Blount, Dion Lewis and James White 12. James White, Julian Edelman, Martellus Bennett, Chris Hogan and Rob Gronkowski 13. New York Jets 14. Martellus Bennett 15. False 16. Matthew Slater 17. Alabama and Rutgers 18. Two 19. a) 6 20. c) 250

Quiz 5: Pot Luck

1. The Patriots' first three Super Bowl appearances were all at the same stadium. Which one?

2. Up to the start of the 2022 season, the Patriots had faced every AFC team in the play-offs bar one. Which one?

3. Tom Brady threw for his 450th touchdown against Baltimore in December 2016. Which receiver caught the 71-yard pass?

4. @BB_HulkSmash is the Twitter handle of which Patriot?

5. Prior to returning to New England in 2012, Josh McDaniels spent a season as offensive coordinator of which NFC team?

6. Which Patriot holds the record for the most career sacks in the play-offs?

7. True or false – While at college, Tom Brady had a part-time job as a sales rep and assistant manager at the university golf course?

8. With the win over Atlanta Bill Belichick became the first head coach with five Super Bowl wins. Which head coach has four Super Bowl wins?

9. Mac Jones threw his first regular season touchdown pass to which receiver?

10. The Patriots won their debut game at Wembley Stadium in London in 2009, thrashing which team 35-7?

11. True or false – Going into Super Bowl LI, Tom Brady had played in more Super Bowls than the players on the Atlanta Falcons roster combined?

12. Whose 78-yard scamper for a touchdown against the Steelers in January 1997 remains the longest postseason run in Patriots history?

13. Which Patriot was a member of the American rugby squad at the 2016 Olympics in Rio?

14. True or false – The Patriots wore white jerseys in all their Super Bowl triumphs?

15. Tom Brady holds the record for the most play-off touchdown passes in NFL history. Who was the previous holder of that record?

16. Who was the first Patriot defender to be inducted into the Pro Football Hall of Fame?

17. Which three members of New England's 2016 roster had brothers who also played in the NFL that year?

18. Which Patriots defender was described by coach Bill Belichick as the 'perfect player' at his 2009 retirement press conference?

19. How many quarterbacks were selected before Tom Brady in the 1999 NFL draft? a) 5 b) 6 c) 7

20. What is the highest number of points that the Patriots have scored in a single quarter? a) 28 b) 31 c) 35

Quiz 4: Answers

1. NRG Stadium, Houston 2. Patriots 34-28 Falcons 3. Tom Brady 4. 25 points 5. True 6. George H. W. Bush and wife Barbara 7. James White 8. Tom Brady 9. Zero 10. James White 11. 20 12. Hamilton 13. Dont'a Hightower 14. Danny Amendola 15. Eric Rowe 16. Malcolm Mitchell, Brandon Bolden, Geneo Grissom, Vincent Valentine and Jonathan Jones 17. Carl Cheffers 18. Lady Gaga 19. c) James White 20. c) 466

Quiz 6: Tom Brady Part 1

1. Brady famously wore what number jersey?

2. In which round of the draft did the Patriots select Brady?

3. Brady missed how many games at the start of the 2016 season following the 'deflategate' ban?

4. Brady played college football for which school?

5. True or false – Brady has never thrown for over 5,000 yards in a single season?

6. Brady threw for a career-best 517 yards in a 38-24 win over which AFC East rival in September 2011?

7. As a youngster, Brady was a fan of which NFL team?

8. After Super Bowl XLIX, Brady gave away his MVP truck to which team mate?

9. In December 2016, Brady recorded his 201st win, breaking the NFL record for the most wins by a quarterback. Which NFC team did the Patriots beat to set the record?

10. Which quarterback's record did Brady surpass on recording his 201st win?

11. In September 2015, Brady tossed his 400th career touchdown pass. Who caught it?

12. In which state was Brady born?

13. True or false – Brady made a cameo appearance in the 2015 movie 'Ocean's 13'?

14. On October 2009 Brady threw six touchdown passes in a shutout rout of which AFC rival?

15. Brady got the starting job in New England after an injury to which quarterback?

16. Who caught more touchdown passes from Brady than any other Patriots receiver?

17. Brady was a highly regarded baseball prospect. Which team drafted him in the 1995 MLB draft?

18. Brady's first ever play-off appearance was a snowy victory over which team?

19. What is the highest number of touchdowns Brady has thrown in a single regular season? a) 48 b) 49 c) 50

20. Brady is one of only two players to have won multiple League and Super Bowl MVP awards. Who is the other? a) John Elway b) Joe Montana c) Terry Bradshaw

Quiz 5: Answers

1. Louisiana Superdome 2. Cincinnati 3. Chris Hogan 4. Brandon Bolden 5. St. Louis Rams 6. Willie McGinest 7. True 8. Chuck Noll 9. Nelson Agholor 10. Tampa Bay Buccaneers 11. True 12. Curtis Martin 13. Nate Ebner 14. False 15. Joe Montana 16. Mike Haynes 17. Chris Long, Devin McCourty and Martellus Bennett 18. Tedy Bruschi 19. b) 6 20. c) 35

Quiz 7: Pot Luck

1. What is the fewest number of games the Patriots have won in a single season?

2. Who was the defensive coordinator on the Patriots' 2016 World Championship-winning team?

3. Tom Brady was one of three starting quarterbacks to win games for the Patriots during the 2016 season. Who were the other two?

4. Up to the start of the 2022 season the Patriots had defeated which three AFC rivals a franchise record four times in the play-offs?

5. Who ran for a touchdown, caught a touchdown and returned a kick for a touchdown in the Patriots' 2016 divisional round win over Houston?

6. Quarterback Mac Jones made his first NFL regular season start against which division rival?

7. Who kicked more play-off extra points in their Patriots career – Stephen Gostkowski or Adam Vinatieri?

8. Which long-time Patriots receiver played on the defensive side of the ball in 2004, collecting three interceptions in the process?

9. True or false – Bill Belichick is the only man in NFL history to have spent more than 20 years as both an assistant coach and a head coach?

10. 'Minitron' was the nickname of which New England stalwart?

11. Which offensive lineman had a 71-yard kick return against the Packers in December 2010?

12. What color jerseys did the Patriots wear in their first Super Bowl appearance?

13. Which defensive back's number 40 jersey has been retired by the Patriots?

14. Coach Belichick holds the NFL record for the most play-off wins by a head coach. Who was the previous holder of that record?

15. Who returned to the sidelines in 2016 after a two-year retirement to become the Patriots' offensive line coach?

16. True or false – The Patriots have appeared in more play-off games under Bill Belichick than all their other coaches combined?

17. Which Patriot holds the record for the most pass attempts in a single game with 70?

18. @Mac_BZ is the Twitter handle of which former Patriots defensive star?

19. In a 1986 game against the Saints, New England endured their worst ever day of rushing. How many yards did their 18 carries produce? a) 2 b) 12 c) 22

20. The mother of which Patriots defender was a reggae singer who topped the charts in Jamaica in the 1980s with a song called 'Girlie, Girlie'? a) Malcolm Butler b) Patrick Chung c) Devin McCourty

Quiz 6: Answers

1. #12 2. Sixth 3. Four 4. University of Michigan 5. False 6. Miami Dolphins 7. San Francisco 49ers 8. Malcolm Butler 9. Los Angeles Rams 10. Peyton Manning 11. Danny Amendola 12. California 13. False 14. Tennessee Titans 15. Drew Bledsoe 16. Rob Gronkowski 17. Montreal Expos 18. Oakland Raiders 19. c) 50 TDs 20. b) Joe Montana

Quiz 8: Rushers

1. Who holds the record for the most playoff touchdowns by a running back in franchise history?

2. With 5,423 yards, who is the Patriots' all-time leading rusher?

3. Who rushed for four touchdowns during a 42-20 rout of the Colts in Indianapolis in November 2014?

4. Which running back also scored four touchdowns against the Colts in a play-off game later that same season?

5. Which versatile running back rushed for 1,199 yards, caught passes for 982 yards and scored 14 TDs in a three-year spell in New England in the early 2010s?

6. Who is the only Patriots running back to have been named a first team All-Pro?

7. In a 2012 game in Buffalo, two New England backs both rushed for over 100 yards. Name the pair.

8. 'Jitterbug' was the nickname of which elusive Patriot running back?

9. Who was the last running back to be taken by the Patriots with their first draft pick?

10. Who are the two Patriots to have had nine 100-yard rushing games in a single season?

11. True or false – The Patriots hold the NFL record for gaining the most rushing yards in a season after racking up a mammoth total of 3,165 yards in 1978?

12. Who holds the Patriots record for the most 100-yard games in a career?

13. The longest running play in franchise history was an 85-yard touchdown scamper against Buffalo in 1961 by which rusher?

14. Who set the record for the most rushing yards in a game with a 212-yard effort against the Jets in September 1983?

15. Which opposition back rushed for 182 yards and a TD in a January 2020 playoff game, the most ever by a running back in a postseason game at Gillette Stadium?

16. Which running back made 194 appearances for the Patriots between 1978 and 1990?

17. Which back rushed for a single-season franchise record 1,635 yards in 2004?

18. In 1996, which back rushed for a touchdown in seven consecutive games?

19. Who is the only Patriot to have won the League rushing title? a) Tony Collins b) Curtis Martin c) Jim Nance

20. LeGarrette Blount rushed for how many touchdowns during the 2016 regular season? a) 16 b) 17 c) 18

Quiz 7: Answers

1. One 2. Matt Patricia 3. Jimmy Garoppolo and Jacoby Brissett 4. Pittsburgh, Jacksonville & Indianapolis 5. Dion Lewis 6. Miami 7. Stephen Gostkowski 8. Troy Brown 9. True 10. Julian Edelman 11. Dan Connolly 12. Red 13. Mike Haynes 14. Tom Landry 15. Dante Scarnecchia 16. True 17. Drew Bledsoe 18. Malcolm Butler 19. a) 2 yards 20. b) Patrick Chung

Quiz 9: Receivers

1. With 672 grabs, who is New England's all-time leading receiver by catches?

2. Who is the only player with over 10,000 receiving yards as a Patriot?

3. The Patriots traded a fourth-round draft pick with which team to acquire the services of Randy Moss?

4. Who are the three Patriots with over 100 catches in a single regular season?

5. Who was the last wide receiver selected by the Patriots with their first pick in the NFL draft?

6. Randy Moss scored a touchdown with a ridiculous one-handed grab against which team in week two of the 2010 season?

7. Two Patriots have over 200 receiving yards in a single game. Wes Welker is one. Which WR, who managed the feat in 1999, is the other?

8. Who are the two Patriots to have caught 16 passes in a single regular season game?

9. In week one of the 2011 season against Miami, Tom Brady threw a 99-yard touchdown pass to which receiver?

10. Which unlikely receiver caught 10 passes as a Patriot, each of which was for a one or two-yard touchdown?

11. Who holds the record for the most touchdown catches by a Patriot in a single season?

12. Who caught more touchdown passes from Tom Brady – Randy Moss or Wes Welker?

13. In a 2012 win over Denver, who became the first Patriot receiver to catch a hat-trick of touchdown pass in a postseason game?

14. Which receiver was drafted in 2003 then went on to spend 15 seasons in New England, making him the longest tenured wide receiver in franchise history?

15. Only one Patriot has led the NFL in catches in a single season. Which one?

16. Prior to Rob Gronkowski who was the last tight end to lead the Patriots in receptions?

17. Who was the Patriots' only 1,000-yard receiver in the 2016 regular season?

18. Who caught the Patriots' only touchdown in their Super Bowl XX loss to the Bears?

19. Wes Welker holds the franchise record for consecutive games with a catch. In how many successive games did he make a grab? a) 83 b) 93 c) 103

20. Who holds the record for the most 100-yard receiving games by a Patriot? a) Troy Brown b) Stanley Morgan c) Wes Welker

Quiz 8: Answers

1. LeGarrette Blount 2. Sam Cunningham 3. Jonas Gray 4. LeGarrette Blount 5. Danny Woodhead 6. Jim Nance 7. Stevan Ridley and Brandon Bolden 8. Dion Lewis 9. Laurence Maroney 10. Curtis Martin and Corey Dillon 11. True 12. Jim Nance 13. Larry Garron 14. Tony Collins 15. Derrick Henry 16. Mosi Tatupu 17. Corey Dillon 18. Curtis Martin 19. c) Jim Nance 20. c) 18

Quiz 10: Pot Luck

1. Which lineman did the Patriots selected with their first pick in the 2022 NFL Draft?

2. The heaviest defeat in franchise history was a 52-0 drubbing in 1972 from which team?

3. The Patriots have an unbeaten play-off record against which three AFC rivals?

4. Which Patriot blocked a punt, blocked a field goal and returned an interception for a touchdown in a Monday Night Football game against the Dolphins in 2010?

5. Who are two Patriots head coaches whose first name and surname start with the same letter?

6. Who are the two Patriots offensive linemen to have had their jersey number retired?

7. True or false – Kicker Adam Vinatieri was a former high school wrestling champion?

8. Tom Brady famously 'fumbled' in the AFC divisional round playoff against Oakland in Jan 2002 but the ruling was overturned because of the 'tuck rule'. Which Raider forced the 'fumble'?

9. Which legendary Patriots receiver was offered a contract with the CFL's British Columbia Lions to play quarterback?

10. Who was the first Patriots punt returner to receive first-team All-Pro recognition?

11. Who holds the record for the most touchdown catches in a single game after grabbing four against Buffalo in 2007?

12. The Patriots' Community Service award is named in honor of which former player?

13. Tom Brady threw five touchdown passes in a single quarter during a 2009 rout of which team?

14. True or false – The Boston Pops Orchestra once played a free concert at Sullivan Stadium?

15. Who was the first New England quarterback to throw for over 400 yards in consecutive games?

16. Tom Brady holds the record for the most Pro Bowl appearances by a Patriot. Who is second on the list after being chosen nine times?

17. What comes next in this sequence and why? 3, 3, 3, 3, 4, 4

18. Which Patriots duo made a cameo appearance in the 2012 movie 'The Three Stooges'?

19. Tom Brady holds the franchise record for the most TD passes in the play-offs. Who is second on that list? a) Drew Bledsoe b) Tony Eason c) Steve Grogan

20. Between 2010 and 2011 Tom Brady set an NFL record by throwing how many passes without an interception? a) 338 b) 348 c) 358

Quiz 9: Answers

1. Wes Welker 2. Stanley Morgan 3. Oakland Raiders 4. Wes Welker, Julian Edelman and Troy Brown 5. N'Keal Harry 6. New York Jets 7. Terry Glenn 8. Troy Brown and Wes Welker 9. Wes Welker 10. Mike Vrabel 11. Randy Moss 12. Randy Moss 13. Rob Gronkowski 14. Troy Brown 15. Wes Welker 16. Ben Coates 17. Julian Edelman 18. Irving Fryar 19. b) 93 20. b) Stanley Morgan

Quiz 11: Rob Gronkowski

1. What was Gronkowski's New England jersey number?

2. Gronk played his college ball at which school?

3. In which round did the Patriots select Gronk in the 2010 NFL Draft?

4. Gronk caught his first regular season touchdown pass against which AFC North team?

5. In which state was Gronk born and raised?

6. True or false – Gronk was selected by the Los Angeles Angels in the 2009 MLB draft?

7. During his Patriots career Gronk caught more touchdown passes against which team than any other?

8. True or false – Gronk has never appeared in all 16 games in a single regular season?

9. What is the name of Rob's brother who joined him on the Patriots active roster in 2011?

10. Gronk is one of three Patriots to have scored at least 10 touchdowns in three successive seasons. Who are the other two?

11. Gronk's longest reception was a 76-yard touchdown grab against which NFC rival in November 2015?

12. In what year was Gronk born?

13. True or false – Ignatius Gronkowski, Rob's great-grandfather, was a member of the US cycling team at the 1924 Olympics?

14. The tight end made a cameo appearance in which 2015 movie?

15. Gronk is one of just two tight ends with 50 touchdown catches in their first five NFL seasons. Who is the other?

16. During his time with the Patriots Gronk caught TD passes from Tom Brady and which other quarterback?

17. In 2011, Gronk set the record for the most touchdown catches in a single regular season by a tight end. How many TD catches did he make?

18. Gronk caught 10 touchdown passes as a rookie, second only to which player turned Super Bowl-winning coach?

19. In 2011, Gronk enjoyed his most prolific regular season. How many catches did he make? a) 87 b) 89 c) 90

20. Only one tight end in NFL history reached 5,000 receiving yards in fewer games than it took Gronk. Which one? a) Antonio Gates b) Shannon Sharpe c) Kellen Winslow

Quiz 10: Answers

1. Cole Strange 2. Miami Dolphins 3. Buffalo, Kansas City and Houston 4. Patrick Chung 5. Bill Belichick and Rod Rust 6. John Hannah and Bruce Armstrong 7. True 8. Charles Woodson 9. Julian Edelman 10. Gunner Olszewski 11. Randy Moss 12. Ron Burton 13. Tennessee Titans 14. True 15. Matt Cassel 16. John Hannah 17. 6 - Super Bowl margins of victory in the Brady/Belichick era 18. Troy Brown and Jerod Mayo 19. b) Tony Eason 20. c) 358

Quiz 12: Pot Luck

1. In 2012, Detroit's Matthew Stafford set the record for the most pass attempts in a season. Which Patriot was the former holder of the record?

2. According to a 2018 headline in the Boston Herald, who is '... the Patriots' Boogeyman'?

3. In 2018, Aaron Rodgers broke Tom Brady's NFL record for the most consecutive passes without an interception. Which former Cleveland Brown was the previous holder of that record before Brady?

4. The Patriots have a losing play-off record against just two AFC rivals. Which two?

5. Which long-time assistant coach was the interim head coach after Dick MacPherson was hospitalized with acute diverticulitis in 1992?

6. In March 2016, the Patriots traded with which team to acquire tight end Martellus Bennett?

7. Tom Brady was 10-0 in his first 10 play-off appearances. Which team brought that streak to an end in the 2005 divisional round?

8. Which Patriots receiver set the record for the longest pass by a non-quarterback in the postseason after throwing a 51-yard strike against the Ravens in January 2015?

9. Who caught that record-breaking pass?

10. In 1978, head coach Chuck Fairbanks controversially left the Patriots to take charge of which college program?

11. Which Patriot holds the NFL record for the most games in a season with at least two touchdown receptions?

12. Who are the six New England head coaches with a better than .500 winning percentage?

13. Which much-traveled kicker was a perfect 12/12 on field goals when replacing the injured Stephen Gostkowski in 2010?

14. Which New England running back had 501 touches between 2008 and 2011 and never lost a fumble?

15. Which undrafted receiver holds the franchise record for the most receiving yards in a single postseason game?

16. True or false – Tom Brady went to the same high school as baseball star Barry Bonds?

17. What is the most games that the Patriots have started the season without a win?

18. Which offensive lineman was awarded the NFL's Ed Block Courage Award in 2011 after overcoming non-Hodgkin's lymphoma?

19. What is the capacity of Gillette Stadium? a) 66,829 b) 68,629 c) 69,929

20. How many games did Tom Brady win in his first 100 home regular season starts? a) 87 b) 88 c) 89

Quiz 11: Answers

1. #87 2. Arizona 3. Second 4. Cincinnati 5. New York 6. False – brother Gordie was drafted in 2006 7. Buffalo 8. False 9. Dan 10. Randy Moss & Corey Dillon 11. New York Giants 12. 1989 13. True 14. Entourage 15. Jimmy Graham 16. Jimmy Garoppolo 17. 17 TDs 18. Mike Ditka 19. c) 90 20. c) Kellen Winslow

Quiz 13: Defense

1. Who is the Patriots' all-time leader in sacks?

2. Who returned an interception for a 47-yard touchdown to give the Patriots their opening score in Super Bowl XXXVI?

3. Who took over as New England's defensive coordinator in 2012?

4. Which linebacker led the Patriots in tackles in eight of his 14 years in New England and was voted to the Pro Bowl in 1980, 1984 and 1985?

5. What is the name of Hall of Famer Howie Long's son, who spent a single season in New England in 2016?

6. Which three-time All-Pro was traded to the Raiders for a 2011 first round draft pick?

7. Which Patriots linebacker returned four interceptions for a touchdown during a stellar career that ran from 1996 through 2008?

8. Which defensive back recorded a sack, seven tackles and two interceptions in Super Bowl XXXIX?

9. Who led the Patriots in sacks in the 2020 season with 5.5?

10. Who were the two Patriot defenders voted to the Pro Bowl for the 2016 season?

11. Which two defensive stars did the Patriots select in the first round of the 2012 draft?

12. True or false – In a division game in 1973 the Patriots allowed the Jets just one completed pass?

13. Who tied a regular season franchise record after recording four sacks against the Jets in November 2011?

14. Which Patriot led the NFL with 10 interceptions in 2006?

15. The franchise record of 36 career interceptions is jointly held by which two defensive backs?

16. Which star linebacker was traded to the Browns for a third-round pick late in the 2016 season?

17. Which linebacker enjoyed a 4.5 sack game during a play-off win against the Jags in January 2006?

18. Which team did the Patriots shut out 27-0 on their run towards Super Bowl LI?

19. What is the fewest number of points allowed by the Patriots in a single 16-game season? a) 237 b) 247 c) 257

20. What is the fewest number of yards allowed by the Patriots defense in a single game? a) 65 b) 75 c) 85

Quiz 12: Answers

1. Drew Bledsoe 2. Tom Coughlin 3. Bernie Kosar 4. Cleveland and Denver 5. Dante Scarnecchia 6. Chicago 7. Denver Broncos 8. Julian Edelman 9. Danny Amendola 10. Colorado 11. Randy Moss 12. Mike Holovak, Chuck Fairbanks, Ron Meyer, Raymond Berry, Pete Carroll and Bill Belichick 13. Shayne Graham 14. BenJarvus Green-Ellis 15. Chris Hogan 16. True 17. Nine 18. Marcus Cannon 19. a) 66,829 20. a) 87

Quiz 14: Tom Brady 2

1. Brady threw six touchdown passes in a blowout 45-10 play-off win in January 2012 against which team?

2. Brady was benched during a shock 2014 loss to which AFC rival?

3. With 632 catches, who holds the record for the most receptions from Brady throws?

4. True or false – Brady has hosted the TV show 'Saturday Night Live'?

5. Brady was on the roster that won the 1997 Rose Bowl. Which future NFL regular was the starting quarterback for Michigan that year?

6. Between 2004 and 2006 Brady dated which famous actress, best known for appearing in cop drama 'Blue Bloods'?

7. Which future media personality was the first tight end to catch a Brady touchdown pass?

8. What nationality is Brady's wife, Gisele?

9. What are Brady's two middle names?

10. In 2001, Brady gained his first reception. Who threw the 23-yard pass?

11. In 2015, Brady added a second reception. Which wide receiver threw this 36-yard pass?

12. Brady made his first NFL start against which AFC rival?

13. True or false – Brady has thrown TD passes to over 60 different receivers?

14. Which first round pick caught Brady's first career touchdown pass?

15. Which former Major League Baseball star is Brady's brother-in-law?

16. With which number pick of the 2000 NFL was Brady selected by the Patriots?

17. Brady suffered more defeats against which opponent while with the Patriots that any other?

18. Who were the six quarterbacks picked before Brady in the 2000 NFL draft?

19. What injury brought Brady's 2008 season to a premature end? a) broken arm b) separated shoulder c) torn ACL

20. Brady was drafted by a Major League Baseball team to play which position? a) catcher b) pitcher c) shortstop

Quiz 13: Answers

1. Andre Tippett 2. Ty Law 3. Matt Patricia 4. Steve Nelson 5. Chris Long 6. Richard Seymour 7. Tedy Bruschi 8. Rodney Harrison 9. Chase Winovich 10. Dont'a Hightower and Devin McCourty 11. Chandler Jones and Dont'a Hightower 12. True 13. Andre Carter 14. Asante Samuel 15. Raymond Clayborn and Ty Law 16. Jamie Collins 17. Willie McGinest 18. Houston Texans 19. a) 237 20. a) 65 yards

Quiz 15: Pot Luck

1. Long-time Patriots offensive coordinator Josh McDaniels had a brief spell as the head coach of which AFC rival?

2. True or false – The Patriots have never lost a regular season game against the Jacksonville Jaguars?

3. True or false – The Patriots won Super Bowl XXVI after losing three of their first four regular season games?

4. How did a Brit called Mark Roberts gain notoriety during the Patriots' Super Bowl win over the Panthers?

5. Who was New England's offensive coordinator on the franchise's first three Super Bowl wins?

6. Who was the defensive coordinator on the Patriots' first three Super Bowl wins?

7. Whose 'wardrobe malfunction' caused controversy during the half-time show at Super Bowl XXXVIII?

8. Who are the three players to have scored over 1,000 regular season points for the Patriots?

9. Who caught fourth quarter touchdown passes for the Rams and Panthers that tied Super Bowls XXXVI and XXXVIII before Adam Vinatieri's last-minute kicks won the games for the Pats?

10. Tom Brady was one of two future Patriots to be drafted in the 1995 MLB draft. Who was the other?

11. Which long-time Patriot is the owner of a racehorse called Undrafted?

12. Who was the last non-kicker to lead the Patriots in season scoring?

13. Who had more wins as head coach of the Patriots – Bill Parcells or Pete Carroll?

14. What is the fishy nickname of former head coach Bill Parcells?

15. The Patriots' record-breaking winning streak in 2003 and 2004 was brought to an end by which team?

16. True or false – O-line coach Dante Scarnecchia has been on the Patriots coaching staff longer than offensive coordinator Josh McDaniels has been alive?

17. Which Patriots legend was involved in a famous locker room bust up with a Boston Globe reporter following a win over the Jets in 1979?

18. Which cornerback returned a blocked field goal for a 62-yard touchdown against Miami in December 2014?

19. Between September and November 2015 the Patriots scored points in how many consecutive quarters? a) 36 b) 37 c) 38

20. In the Brady / Belichick era, how many points have the Patriots scored in the first quarter of all their Super Bowl appearances combined? a) 0 b) 10 c) 21

Quiz 14: Answers

1. Denver Broncos 2. Kansas City Chiefs 3. Wes Welker 4. True 5. Brian Griese 6. Bridget Moynahan 7. Jermaine Wiggins 8. Brazilian 9. Edward Patrick 10. Kevin Faulk 11. Danny Amendola 12. Indianapolis Colts 13. True 14. Terry Glenn 15. Kevin Youkilis 16. Pick 199 17. Miami 18. Chad Pennington, Giovanni Carmazzi, Chris Redman, Tee Martin, Marc Bulger and Spergon Wynn 19. c) Torn ACL 20. a) Catcher

Quiz 16: Special Teams

1. Who is New England's all-time leading points scorer?

2. How long was the Adam Vinatieri field goal that won Super Bowl XXXVI against the Rams?

3. The famous 'Snowplow' game saw the Patriots defeat which team 3-0 thanks to a controversial late field goal?

4. Who holds the record for the most kick-off returns by a Patriot?

5. Who are the two New England kickers to be named First Team All-Pros?

6. Who returned a kick-off 98 yards for a touchdown in the Patriots' 2016 Divisional Round play-off win against Houston?

7. Whose 93-yard boot against the Bills 1991 is the longest punt in franchise history?

8. Who returned a punt for a 55-yard touchdown against the Steelers in the AFC Championship game in January 2002?

9. Whose 94-yard touchdown against Miami in January 2011 is the longest punt return in franchise history?

10. Which Patriots quarterback converted the NFL's first drop kick since the 1940s during a 2006 win over the Dolphins?

11. What was the name of New England's barefoot kicker who was selected for the Pro Bowl in 1986?

12. Who took a kick-off to the house for an NFL record 108-yard touchdown against the Jets in September 2011?

13. Which defensive tackle blocked two field goals in a 2000 win over the Buffalo Bills?

14. Which defensive back scored three kick-off-return touchdowns during his rookie season in 1977?

15. Which kicker-cum-receiver finished as the AFL's all-time leader in points and field goals?

16. In 1983, who became the first Patriots punter elected to the Pro Bowl?

17. Who are the three Patriots to have returned at least three punts for a touchdown?

18. What was the name of the Englishman who was New England's kicker from 1974 to 1983?

19. Up to the close of the 2020 season, what was the longest field goal in franchise history? a) 60 yards b) 61 yards c) 62 yards

20. Stephen Gostkowski holds the NFL record for the most PATs converted in succession. How many successful kicks in a row did he make? a) 512 b) 523 c) 533

Quiz 15: Answers

1. Denver 2. False 3. True 4. He streaked 5. Charlie Weis 6. Romeo Crennel 7. Janet Jackson 8. Gino Cappelletti, Adam Vinatieri and Stephen Gostkowski 9. Ricky Proehl 10. Lawyer Milloy 11. Wes Welker 12. BenJarvus Green-Ellis 13. Bill Parcells 14. Tuna 15. Pittsburgh Steelers 16. False 17. Raymond Clayborn 18. Kyle Arrington 19. c) 38 quarters 20. a) 0

Quiz 17: 1960s

1. In which year did the Patriots make their professional debut?

2. Who was the head coach in the Patriots' debut season?

3. Who took over head coaching duties in the middle of the 1961 season and remained in charge until 1968?

4. On what day of the week did the Patriots play their home games in their first AFL season?

5. The Patriots were routed 51-10 by which team in the 1963 AFL Championship game?

6. What was the name of the owner who founded the Patriots franchise?

7. The Patriots' first regular season game was a 13-10 loss to which team?

8. Which stadium hosted that historic first game?

9. A fumble return for a touchdown gave the Patriots their maiden win. Which team did they beat?

10. The then biggest winning margin of victory in franchise history was recorded in a 41-0 rout of which team in December 1961?

11. Which Patriots linebacker, drafted in 1962, played in five AFL All-Star Games and was inducted into the Pro Football Hall of Fame in 2001?

12. In 1967, the Patriots faced NFL opposition for the first time. They lost 33-3 in a pre-season game against which team?

13. 'Earthquake' was the nickname of which defensive tackle who was inducted into the Patriots Hall of Fame in 1993?

14. True or false – The Patriots played games at Fenway Park in the 1960s?

15. Despite just three points being scored in the opening quarter, the Patriots shared a 43-43 tie with which team in October 1964?

16. In 1967, which Patriot became the first running back to rush for over 1,000 yards in successive AFL seasons?

17. Who intercepted 29 passes during a Patriots career that stretched from 1961 through to 1967?

18. Who was appointed head coach in January 1969?

19. Why is Phil Bissell important in Patriots folklore? a) he scored the team's first points b) he designed the team's original logo c) he was the announcer on the team's first win

20. By what nickname was quarterback Vito Parilli better known? a) Babe b) Ice c) Duke

Quiz 16: Answers

1. Stephen Gostkowski 2. 48 yards 3. Miami Dolphins 4. Kevin Faulk 5. Adam Vinatieri and Stephen Gostkowski 6. Dion Lewis 7. Shawn McCarthy 8. Troy Brown 9. Julian Edelman 10. Doug Flutie 11. Tony Franklin 12. Ellis Hobbs 13. Chad Eaton 14. Raymond Clayborn 15. Gino Cappelletti 16. Rich Camarillo 17. Julian Edelman, Irving Fryar and Troy Brown 18. John Smith 19. c) 62 yards 20. b) 523

Quiz 18: 1970s

1. In what year did the Boston Patriots become the New England Patriots?

2. Which brewery gave its name to the Patriots' first purpose-built stadium?

3. Which quarterback did the Patriots select with the first overall pick of the 1971 draft?

4. True or false – the Patriots rushed for over 3,000 yards in the 1978 regular season?

5. Who was the team's head coach from 1973 through to 1978?

6. Patriots stalwarts John Hannah, Sam Cunningham and Darryl Stingley were all taken in the first round of which year's NFL Draft?

7. Which legendary Patriots defensive back had eight interceptions as a rookie in 1976?

8. Who was the only Patriot to have a 1,000-yard rushing season during the 1970s?

9. Which Patriots tight end went to the Pro Bowl in 1976, 1977 and 1978?

10. The Patriots had their first two 1,000-yard receivers in 1979. Name the speedy duo.

11. The Patriots suffered a last-minute 24-21 wild card round defeat in 1976 to which eventual Super Bowl winner?

12. Which quarterback rushed for a record 12 touchdowns during the 1976 regular season?

13. In what year did the Patriots claim their first outright divisional title?

14. The Patriots thrashed which division rival by a then record scoreline of 56 to 3 in September 1979?

15. Which fan-favorite Patriots linebacker recovered three fumbles during a game against Philadelphia in 1978?

16. True or false – In a game against the Steelers in 1976, the Patriots recovered six opposition fumbles?

17. Which diminutive running back holds the franchise record for the most all-purpose yards in a season, after racking up 2,444 of them in 1974?

18. John Hannah was one of two Patriots offensive linemen to receive first team All-Pro honors in the 1970s. Who was the other?

19. What was the nickname of running back Bob Gladieux? a) Groucho b) Harpo c) Zeppo

20. The Patriots set a franchise record for fumbles in 1973. How many times did they put the ball on the ground? a) 33 b) 43 c) 53

Quiz 17: Answers

1. 1960 2. Lou Saban 3. Mike Holovak 4. Friday 5. San Diego Chargers 6. Billy Sullivan 7. Denver Broncos 8. B.U. Field 9. New York Titans 10. San Diego Chargers 11. Nick Buoniconti 12. Baltimore Colts 13. Jim Lee Hunt 14. True 15. Oakland Raiders 16. Jim Nance 17. Ron Hall 18. Mike Rush 19. b) he designed the team's first logo 20. a) Babe

Quiz 19: 1980s

1. In 1982, a non-player called Mark Henderson secured his place in Patriots folklore. Why?

2. Which noted disciplinarian succeeded Ron Erhardt as head coach in 1982?

3. Which quarterback did the Patriots select with the 15th pick of the 1983 NFL draft?

4. In 1983, who became only the third running back in franchise history to rush for over 1,000 yards in a season?

5. The Patriots used the first overall pick in the 1984 draft to select which mercurial wide receiver?

6. New England defeated which opponent on the road for the first time since 1969 in the 1985 AFC Championship game?

7. Which team did the Patriots face in Super Bowl XX?

8. Which head coach steered the Patriots to their first AFC title?

9. Who rushed for a career-best 1,227 yards in the 1985 regular season?

10. True or false – The Patriots GM got involved in a fist fight with two Los Angeles players following a 1985 divisional round play-off win over the Raiders?

11. Which Patriot was named AFC Defensive Player of the Year in 1985?

12. Which high profile businessman bought the Patriots franchise in 1986?

13. Whose number 57 jersey number was retired in 1987 following a 14-year career with the Patriots?

14. Which defensive back's streak of 161 consecutive games played came to an end when he couldn't face the Eagles in November 1987?

15. Who caught his 500th career pass in a game against the Seahawks in December 1988?

16. Which 13-year Patriot and special team player extraordinaire went to the Pro Bowl for the only time in 1986?

17. What was long-time quarterback Steve Grogan's jersey number?

18. Which Patriots rookie running back received Pro Bowl recognition for the only time in his career in 1988?

19. How many AFC East titles did the Patriots win during the 1980s? a) one b) two c) three

20. Which divisional rival did the Patriots defeat to claim their first NFL play-off win? a) Buffalo Bills b) Miami Dolphins c) New York Jets

Quiz 18: Answers

1. 1971 2. Schaefer 3. Jim Plunkett 4. True 5. Chuck Fairbanks 6. 1973 7. Mike Haynes 8. Sam Cunningham 9. Russ Francis 10. Harold Jackson and Stanley Morgan 11. Oakland Raiders 12. Steve Grogan 13. 1978 14. New York Jets 15. Steve Nelson 16. True 17. Mack Herron 18. Leon Gray 19. b) Harpo 20. c) 53

Quiz 20: 1990s

1. The decade got off to a woeful start in 1990 as the Patriots recorded their worst ever regular season record. Who was the coach that year?

2. What major change was made to the field at Foxboro Stadium in 1991?

3. In what year did the Patriots change from red to blue home uniforms?

4. Which quarterback did the Patriots select with the first overall pick of the 1993 draft?

5. In 1994, who became the fourth owner of the Patriots franchise?

6. The Patriots defeated which team 20-6 in the AFC Championship to reach Super Bowl XXXI?

7. Which team did the Patriots face in Super Bowl XXXI?

8. Who stepped down as New England head coach in January 1997?

9. In December 1996 the Patriots overturned a 22-point deficit to famously beat which NFC rival 23-22 and in the process secure a first home play-off game in a decade?

10. Who rushed for 3,799 yards in his three years with the Patriots between 1995 and 1997?

11. Which Patriot set a then NFL record after grabbing 90 receptions during the 1996 season?

12. Which tight end led the Patriots in receptions for five seasons during the 1990s?

13. Between September 1989 and November 1993 New England lost nine matches in a row against which divisional rival?

14. What was Drew Bledsoe's jersey number?

15. Only one Patriot returned a kick-off for a touchdown in the 1990s. Which diminutive returner went to the house with 99 and 100-yard returns in 1991 and 1992?

16. Which Patriot led the league with nine interceptions in 1998?

17. Who was the Patriots head coach during the 1997, 1998 and 1999 seasons?

18. Two Patriots were named Associated Press Offensive Rookie of the Year in the 1990s. Which two?

19. The lowest recorded attendance for a Patriots game was set in 1991. How many saw the season finale against the Colts? a) 19,131 b) 20,131 c) 21,131

20. In 1990, the Patriots set the NFL record for the fewest points scored in a season. How many did they score? a) 181 b) 191 c) 201

Quiz 19: Answers

1. He was driving the plow in the infamous Snowplow Game 2. Ron Meyer 3. Tony Eason 4. Tony Collins 5. Irving Fryar 6. Miami Dolphins 7. Chicago Bears 8. Raymond Berry 9. Craig James 10. True 11. Andre Tippett 12. Victor Kiam 13. Steve Nelson 14. Raymond Clayborn 15. Stanley Morgan 16. Mosi Tatupu 17. #14 18. John Stephens 19. a) One 20. c) New York Jets

Quiz 21: 2000s – The Glory Years

1. By what name was the Patriots' home stadium known before Gillette bought the naming rights?

2. Who led the Patriots with 1,157 yards rushing and 12 touchdowns in their 2001 championship season?

3. Who threw a touchdown pass, caught a touchdown and ran for a touchdown in the Patriots' 38-17 win over the Colts in October 2001?

4. The Patriots marked the opening of Gillette Stadium with 30-14 over which AFC rival?

5. In 2004 who set the franchise record for the most rushing yards in a season?

6. Who scored the Patriots' only offensive touchdown in the Super Bowl XXXVI win over the Rams?

7. Which receiver caught 10 passes for 143 yards and a touchdown in the Super Bowl XXXVIII win over Carolina?

8. How long was Adam Vinatieri's field goal that won Super Bowl XXXVIII for New England?

9. Who were the first team to beat the Patriots in an AFC Championship game?

10. Which two Patriots caught touchdown passes in both Super Bowl XXXVIII and Super Bowl XXXIX?

11. Only one Patriot who started Super Bowl XXXIX had a surname that started with a vowel. Who was it? (clue – it was an o-lineman)

12. In 2006, who grabbed his 535th catch to become the Patriots' then all-time leading receiver?

13. Which team did the Patriots defeat 21-12 in the 2007 AFC Championship game?

14. Which Patriot led the NFL in receptions in 2007 and 2009 after grabbing 112 and 123 respectively?

15. In which city did the Patriots win Super Bowl XXXIX against the Eagles?

16. Whose total of 12,349 all-purpose yards, compiled between 1999 and 2011, is a franchise record?

17. Which running back rushed for a touchdown in six successive games in 2009?

18. True or false – Between 2000 and 2003 the Patriots won an NFL record eight successive overtime games?

19. Including the play-offs, how many successive games did the Patriots win between October 2003 and October 2004? a) 19 b) 20 c) 21

20. The Patriots hold the NFL record for the most consecutive play-off wins. How many did they win between 2002 and 2006? a) 10 b) 11 c) 12

Quiz 20: Answers

1. Rod Rust 2. Astroturf was replaced by natural grass 3. 1993 4. Drew Bledsoe 5. Robert Kraft 6. Jacksonville 7. Green Bay Packers 8. Bill Parcells 9. New York Giants 10. Curtis Martin 11. Terry Glenn 12. Ben Coates 13. Miami Dolphins 14. #11 15. Jon Vaughn 16. Ty Law 17. Pete Carroll 18. Leonard Russell and Curtis Martin 19. b) 20,131 20. a) 181

Quiz 22: 2010s

1. In October 2010, the Patriots scored rushing, receiving, kick return, interception return and blocked field goal return touchdowns during a 41-14 rout of which divisional rival?

2. The word 'buttfumble' entered the NFL lexicon courtesy of a mishap by which quarterback against the Patriots in 2012?

3. Tom Brady threw for a career-best 517 yards during a 38-24 rout of which team in September 2011?

4. The Patriots reached Super Bowl XLVI after sneaking past which team 23-20 in the AFC Championship game?

5. Between 2010 & 2020, the Patriots had three 1,000-yard rushers. BenJarvus Green-Ellis & LeGarrette Blount were 2. Who was the third?

6. Which defensive back tied for the League lead after grabbing seven interceptions in 2011?

7. Which defensive back returned a kick-off 104 yards for a touchdown against the Jets in October 2012?

8. The Patriots chose defensive tackles with their number one draft pick in both 2014 and 2015. Which two players did they select?

9. In a 2014 game against the Colts, who became the first Patriot to rush for over 100 yards in both halves of the same game?

10. Which Patriot set the record for the most receptions by a running back in a Super Bowl after grabbing 14 catches against Atlanta in Super Bowl LI?

11. At Super Bowl XLIX Tom Brady became the third quarterback to win four Super Bowls. Who are the other two QBs with four wins?

12. Who, in his single season with the Patriots in 2014, was voted to the Pro Bowl, named a first-team All-Pro and won a Super Bowl ring?

13. The Patriots routed which team 45-7 in the AFC Championship game to secure their place in Super Bowl XLIX?

14. What was the final score in Super Bowl XLIX against the Seahawks?

15. Tom Brady threw TD passes to four different receivers in Super Bowl XLIX. Name the quartet.

16. What stadium hosted Super Bowl XLIX?

17. The Patriots were beaten by which team in the 2013 and 2015 AFC Championship Game?

18. Which two starters against Seattle in Super Bowl XLIX had first names and surnames that start with the same letter? (Clue, they're both on defense)

19. In 2010, the Patriots tied the NFL record for the fewest turnovers in a single season. How many times did they give up the ball? a) 10 b) 11 c) 12

20. Three-year Patriot punter Zoltan Mesko was born in which country? a) Bulgaria b) Poland c) Romania

Quiz 21: Answers

1. CMGI Field 2. Antowain Smith 3. David Patten 4. Pittsburgh 5. Corey Dillon 6. David Patten 7. Deion Branch 8. 41 yards 9. Indianapolis Colts 10. David Givens and Mike Vrabel 11. Joe Andruzzi 12. Troy Brown 13. San Diego 14. Wes Welker 15. Jacksonville 16. Kevin Faulk 17. Laurence Maroney 18. True 19. c) 21 games 20. a) 10

Quiz 23: Pot Luck

1. What number jersey did Randy Moss wear at the Patriots?

2. In 1985, which linebacker became the first Patriot to record two safeties in a single season?

3. Between 1984 and 1998 the Patriots lost 10 successive games against which opponent?

4. Between Dec 2003 and Dec 2010 New England won 15 consecutive games against which AFC rival?

5. Which team defeated the Patriots in Super Bowls XLII and XLVI?

6. True or False – Former Patriots receiver Randy Moss is the brother of former Washington receiver Santana Moss?

7. Which team did the Patriots defeat in their final game at Foxboro Stadium in January 2002?

8. After Corey Dillon in 2004, who was the next Patriot to rush for over 1,000 yards in a season?

9. Who holds the record for the most sacks by a Patriot in a single season?

10. True or false – Shaq Mason's full name is Shaquille Olajuwon Mason?

11. Devin McCourty is one of only three players in NFL history to have won All-Pro honors at both safety and cornerback. Who are the other two?

12. Who were the two Patriots selected to the NFL's 75th anniversary team?

13. Which broadcaster, who called 743 New England games, was known as 'The Voice of the Patriots'?

14. True or false – Tom Brady was sacked on the first play from scrimmage in his first regular season start?

15. Who was the MVP in the Patriots' Super Bowl XXXIX triumph over the Eagles?

16. Tom Brady has accumulated the most passing yards for the Patriots. Who is second on that list?

17. Which former Patriot can be found on Twitter with the account @MartysaurusRex?

18. True or false – In a 2008 game against the Rams the Patriots failed to give up a single penalty?

19. Who was the first Patriot to throw for over 300 yards and rush for over 50 yards in the same game? a) Tom Brady b) Matt Cassel c) Steve Grogan

20. Which Patriots defensive lineman was the unlikely scorer of the first touchdown in the history of the AFL? a) Bob Bee b) Bob Dee c) Bob Mee

Quiz 22: Answers

1. Miami 2. Mark Sanchez 3. Miami 4. Baltimore 5. Stevan Ridley 6. Kyle Arrington 7. Devin McCourty 8. Dominique Easley & Malcolm Brown 9. Jonas Gray 10. James White 11. Bradshaw & Montana 12. Darrelle Revis 13. Indianapolis 14. 28-24 15. LaFell, Gronkowski, Amendola, Edelman 16. University of Phoenix Stadium 17. Denver 18. Brandon Browner and Sealver Siliga 19. a) 10 20. c) Romania

Quiz 24: The Numbers Game

What number jersey did the following players wear?

1. Danny Amendola and Troy Brown

2. Martellus Bennett and Terry Glenn

3. Cyrus Jones and Ty Law

4. Rich Camarillo and Stephen Gostkowski

5. Tedy Bruschi and Dont'a Hightower

6. Tony Eason and Julian Edelman

7. Tony Collins and Dion Lewis

8. Zoltan Mesko and Steve Grogan

9. Matt Cassel and Scott Zolak

10. Curtis Martin and Corey Dillon

11. Jonathan Freeny and Willie McGinest

12. Jim Nance and Jonas Gray

13. Vincent Brisby and Daniel Graham

14. Chandler Jones and Roman Phifer

15. Raymond Clayborn and Logan Ryan

16. LeGarrette Blount and Harold Jackson

17. Stanley Morgan and David Patten

18. Joe Andruzzi and Dan Connolly

19. Rob Ninkovich and Mike Vrabel

20. Brian Holloway and Sebastian Vollmer

Quiz 23: Answers

1. #81 2. Don Blackmon 3. Denver 4. Buffalo 5. New York Giants 6. False 7. Oakland 8. BenJarvus Green-Ellis 9. Andre Tippett 10. True 11. Rod Woodson and Ronnie Lott 12. John Hannah and Mike Haynes 13. Gil Santos 14. True 15. Deion Branch 16. Drew Bledsoe 17. Martellus Bennett 18. True 19. b) Matt Cassel 20. b) Bob Dee

Quiz 25: Anagrams

Re-arrange the letters to make the name of a present or former Patriot.

1. MY BAD ROT

2. SAD MR NOSY

3. JUNE LED ANIMAL

4. OWL INSIDE

5. WOK THINS GEEK SPOT

6. BRUTAL CELL MOM

7. DITSY CHERUB

8. FUNK VIA ELK

9. ANY MADDEN LOAN

10. MOAN STRANGELY

11. LEWD BED SORE

12. WRONG BOOK IRKS

13. ILLICIT NEW GEMS

14. NEVER GO STAG

15. PATTERNED PIT

16. BIKE MARVEL

17. MR DEVOUT CYNIC

18. GET TURNTABLE ROLE

19. DATES LONER

20. BLAST METER TUNNEL

Quiz 24: Answers

1. #80 2. #88 3. #24 4. #3 5. #54 6. #11 7. #33 8. #14 9. #16 10. #28 11. #55 12. #35 13. #82 14. #95 15. #26 16. #29 17. #86 18. #63 19. #50 20. #76

Quiz 26: Pot Luck

1. What color is the facemask on the Patriots helmet?

2. Which Patriot had the best-selling jersey in the NFL in 2018?

3. What is the only franchise the Patriots have defeated twice in the Super Bowl?

4. True or false – The last tied game involving the Patriots was in the 1960s?

5. Which legendary Patriots linebacker picked off a Donovan McNabb pass in the closing stages of Super Bowl XXXIX to ice the win for New England?

6. Geographically, what is the closest AFC team to the Patriots?

7. What is the name of New England's mascot?

8. Which receiver threw a 25-yard touchdown pass in an October 2021 game against the Jets?

9. Who caught that trick-play pass?

10. Which Patriots defender, who played for the team between 1995 and 2004, was voted into the Pro Football Hall of Fame in 2019?

11. True or false – The Patriots are unbeaten in games at Gillette Stadium when they've had the lead at half time?

12. The Patriots acquired Jason McCourty following a 2018 trade with which team?

13. Which Patriots back holds the NFL record for the most rushing touchdowns by a rookie in a single postseason?

14. True or false – Tom Brady has made more Super Bowl appearances than any other player in NFL history?

15. Who was the last New England quarterback other than Tom Brady to be elected to the Pro Bowl?

16. A road trip of over 3,000 miles ensues when the Patriots are away at which three opponents?

17. Whose 66 rushing yards against the Bills in December 2018 are the most in a single game by a wide receiver in franchise history?

18. Which New England receiver started his college career playing lacrosse before transferring to Monmouth to play football?

19. In a 2019 auction a rare Tom Brady trading card sold for what record-breaking amount? a) $200,100 b) $300,100 c) $400,100

20. What number jersey did long-time New England defensive star Vince Wilfork wear? a) #74 b) #75 c) #76

Quiz 25: Answers

1. Tom Brady 2. Randy Moss 3. Julian Edelman 4. Dion Lewis 5. Stephen Gostkowski 6. Malcolm Butler 7. Tedy Bruschi 8. Kevin Faulk 9. Danny Amendola 10. Stanley Morgan 11. Drew Bledsoe 12. Rob Gronkowski 13. Willie McGinest 14. Steve Grogan 15. Andre Tippett 16. Mike Vrabel 17. Devin McCourty 18. LeGarrette Blount 19. Nate Solder 20. Martellus Bennett

Quiz 27: Super Bowl LIII

1. Which team did the Patriots face in Super Bowl LIII?

2. What was the final score in the game?

3. Who was named the game's Most Valuable Player?

4. Which Patriot scored the only touchdown in Super Bowl LIII?

5. Super Bowl LIII was hosted in which stadium?

6. Did the Patriots wear home or road uniforms at Super Bowl LIII?

7. True or false – Tom Brady's first pass at Super Bowl LIII resulted in an interception?

8. The longest pass of Super Bowl LIII was a 29 yarder from Tom Brady to which receiver?

9. Who was the only Patriot to record over 100 receiving yards during Super Bowl LIII?

10. Which Patriot intercepted a pass during Super Bowl LIII?

11. Tom Brady became the oldest quarterback to lead his team to Super Bowl victory. Who was the previous holder of that record?

12. True or false – Super Bowl LIII was the lowest-scoring Super Bowl of all time?

13. Tom Brady became the first player with six Super Bowl wins. He was previously tied with which defensive star with five?

14. What was the score at half-time?

15. Who was the referee at Super Bowl LIII?

16. The daughter of which civil rights movement leader performed the coin toss?

17. Which singer performed the National Anthem at Super Bowl LIII?

18. Which group headlined the half-time show at Super Bowl LIII?

19. How old was Bill Belichick at Super Bowl LIII? a) 64 b) 65 c) 66

20. How old was Tom Brady at Super Bowl LIII? a) 40 b) 41 c) 42

Quiz 26: Answers

1. Red 2. Tom Brady 3. The Rams 4. True 5. Tedy Bruschi 6. New York Jets 7. Pat Patriot 8. Kendrick Bourne 9. Nelson Agholor 10. Ty Law 11. False – They've lost one 12. Cleveland 13. Sony Michel 14. True 15. Drew Bledsoe 16. Oakland, San Francisco and Seattle 17. Cordarrelle Patterson 18. Chris Hogan 19. c) $400,100 20. b) #75

Quiz 28: Pot Luck

1. Who was the defensive play caller on New England's 2018 World Championship-winning team?

2. What color is the New England helmet?

3. True or False – New England punter Jake Bailey is the brother of long-time NFL kicker Dan Bailey?

4. The Patriots are one of just three teams to win the Super Bowl a year after a Super Bowl loss. Who are the other two teams to do so?

5. Which two New England defensive backs started every game during the 2018 World Championship season?

6. Bill Belichick became the oldest head coach to win a Super Bowl after the Super Bowl LIII victory. Who was the previous holder of that record?

7. Which two Patriots played both offensive and defensive snaps during the 2018 season?

8. The Patriots sent a 2018 draft pick to which team to acquire the services of Cordarrelle Patterson?

9. True or false – There were six players on the Patriots roster at Super Bowl LIII who were older than opposition head coach Sean McVay?

10. Which Patriot won the AP Defensive Rookie of the Year award for 2008?

11. Which former Patriot rusher appears on Twitter under the handle @flyguy2stackz?

12. Which former New England quarterback is now the owner of the Doubleback Winery in Washington?

13. True or false – The Patriots hold the record for scoring the most points in a Super Bowl while still losing?

14. What was the only NFC team to defeat the Patriots during the 2018 season?

15. Which former Patriots coordinator was the head coach of the team that delivered that sole NFC defeat?

16. Tom Brady was unbeaten in his Patriots career in games against which NFC East opponent?

17. Which receiver caused San Diego's Marlon McCree to fumble during an interception return to give the Patriots fresh hope in the closing stages of the 2006 Divisional playoff game?

18. Which Hawaii guard was the first player drafted by the Patriots in the Bill Belichick era?

19. How many of New England's Super Bowl LIII roster had previously appeared in a Super Bowl? a) 18 b) 28 c) 38

20. Between 1990 and 2014 the Patriots earned a first-round playoff bye how many times? a) 10 b) 12 c) 14

Quiz 27: Answers

1. Los Angeles Rams 2. Patriots 13-3 Rams 3. Julian Edelman 4. Sony Michel 5. Mercedes-Benz Stadium, Atlanta 6. Road 7. True 8. Rob Gronkowski 9. Julian Edelman 10. Stephon Gilmore 11. Peyton Manning 12. True 13. Charles Haley 14. Patriots 3-0 Rams 15. John Parry 16. Bernice King, daughter of Martin Luther King 17. Gladys Knight 18. Maroon 5 19. c) 66 20. b) 41

Quiz 29: 2018 World Champions

1. The Patriots finished the regular season with what record?

2. With 931 yards who led the team in rushing in 2018?

3. Who led the team in touchdowns in 2018 with five rushing and seven receiving scores?

4. Whose 850 receiving yards were the most by a Patriot during 2018?

5. Who was the only Patriot to return a kickoff for a touchdown in 2018?

6. Which defensive lineman led the team in sacks in 2018 with 7.5?

7. Who returned a blocked punt 29 yards for a touchdown during a 38-31 win over the Bears in week seven?

8. Which defensive back led the team in interceptions with four?

9. Tom Brady was one of three Patriots to throw a pass during the 2018 regular season. Who were the other two?

10. Who returned a pick 84 yards for a score against the Bills in week eight?

11. Whose 63-yard reception against Pittsburgh was the longest touchdown catch by a Patriot during the 2018 regular season?

12. Whose total of eight rushing yards during the 2018 regular season included four touchdown runs?

13. The Patriots defeated which team in the Divisional round playoff?

14. New England reached Super Bowl LIII after beating which team in the AFC Championship game?

15. What was the final score in that epic AFC Championship decider?

16. Whose two-yard touchdown run in overtime clinched the AFC Championship for the Patriots?

17. Who scored New England's only receiving touchdown in the AFC title game?

18. Who was the only Patriot to receive First-Team All-Pro honors in 2018?

19. How many points did the Patriots score during the 2018 regular season? a) 416 b) 426 c) 436

20. How many points did the Patriots concede during the 2018 regular season? a) 315 b) 325 c) 335

Quiz 28: Answers

1. Brian Flores 2. Silver 3. False 4. Dallas and Miami 5. Stephon Gilmore and Devin McCourty 6. Tom Coughlin 7. Josh Gordon and Rob Gronkowski 8. Oakland 9. True 10. Jerod Mayo 11. Sony Michel 12. Drew Bledsoe 13. True 14. Detroit 15. Matt Patricia 16. Dallas 17. Troy Brown 18. Adrian Klemm 19. c) 38 20. c) 14

Quiz 30: Pot Luck

1. Which New England linebacker recorded two sacks in Super Bowl LIII?

2. Prior to the 2020 season, in what year were the Patriots last swept by an AFC East opponent?

3. What color are the pants in New England's home uniform?

4. Which defensive back returned a Ben Roethlisberger pass 87 yards for a score in the January 2005 AFC Championship decider?

5. Who was the only Patriot who started Super Bowl LIII whose first name and surname began with the same letter?

6. True or false – Up to and including the 2018 season the Patriots were 39-0 against AFC opponents in home games where both Tom Brady and Julian Edelman played?

7. How many home games did the Patriots lose during their 2018 World Championship season?

8. Tom Brady is one of only two players in NFL history to have started over 200 regular season and 25 playoff games. Who is the other?

9. The Patriots claimed their first Super Bowl triumph wearing what color jerseys?

10. True or false – Tom Brady is the only quarterback to throw for over 500 yards in a single Super Bowl?

11. Which team did the Patriots face in their first ever NFL playoff game?

12. Who was the only player to appear in Super Bowl LIII who also played in the previous Super Bowl between the Rams and Patriots?

13. Which Patriots running back won the AP Offensive Rookie of the Year Award for 1988?

14. Which two former Patriots faced off against New England in Super Bowl LIII?

15. Which Patriots great shares his name with a Scottish actor who stars as Holden Radcliffe in the TV drama 'Marvel's Agents of S.H.I.E.L.D'?

16. Before Sony Michel, who was the last running back selected by the Patriots in the first round of the NFL Draft?

17. Do the Patriots have a winning or losing overall record in Thursday Night Games?

18. Which Patriots offensive stalwart played defensive end at college before converting to offense during a spell in the Arena League?

19. The first Patriots logo featured what? a) a rifle b) a ship c) a tri-cornered hat

20. Approximately what percentage of tickets for Super Bowl LIII was awarded to the Patriots? a) 17.5% b) 22.5% c) 27.5%

Quiz 29: Answers

1. 11 wins 5 losses 2. Sony Michel 3. James White 4. Julian Edelman 5. Cordarrelle Patterson 6. Trey Flowers 7. Kyle Van Noy 8. Duron Harmon 9. Brian Hoyer and Julian Edelman 10. Devin McCourty 11. Chris Hogan 12. James Develin 13. L.A. Chargers 14. Kansas City 15. Patriots 37-31 Chiefs 16. Rex Burkhead 17. Phillip Dorsett 18. Stephon Gilmore 19. c) 436 20. b) 325

Quiz 31: Offensive Aces

1. Which offensive all-rounder rushed for 3,607 yards and caught 431 passes for another 3,701 yards in his 13-year New England career?

2. Before Mac Jones in 2021, who was the last quarterback selected by the Patriots in the first round of the NFL Draft?

3. With 87 catches, who led the team in receptions during the 2018 World Championship-winning season?

4. Legendary Patriots receiver Wes Welker spent the final season of his NFL career with which NFC team?

5. Which incredibly tough guard missed just 5 games through injury in a 13-year career that stretched from 1973 through to 1985?

6. Who is the only New England tight end with 10 or more touchdown receptions in a single season?

7. Which versatile receiver caught 557 passes in a 15-year career with the Patriots that ran from 1993 to 2007?

8. Who scored an incredible 47 touchdowns during a three-year spell in New England between 2007 and 2009?

9. Which legendary tackle appeared for the Patriots in the 1980s, 1990s and 2000s?

10. Which receiver caught eight passes for 152 yards during the Super Bowl LII loss to the Eagles?

11. Who is the only Patriot to rush for over 1,000 yards in three different seasons?

12. Which explosive Patriot was the first player in team history to top 1,000 receiving yards in a season three times?

13. Which offensive guard went to the Pro Bowl six times between 2007 and 2013?

14. In 2013, who became the third Patriot in team history to catch over 100 passes in a single season?

15. Which tight end caught just 10 passes in his 1991 rookie season but later went to five Pro Bowls and was twice named a First-Team All-Pro?

16. Who is the only New England rusher to break the 1,500-yard barrier in a single regular season?

17. Who was the first Patriots quarterback to throw a touchdown pass in the Super Bowl?

18. Which New England rusher was the first player to record back-to-back 1,000-yard rushing seasons?

19. Star rusher LeGarrette Blount had two spells in New England. He spent a season with which team in between those two spells? a) Philadelphia b) Pittsburgh c) Tampa Bay

20. Which of the following receivers had the most passing yards while with the Patriots? a) Irving Fryar b) Terry Glenn c) Randy Moss

Quiz 30: Answers

1. Dont'a Hightower 2. 2000 3. Navy blue 4. Rodney Harrison 5. Jonathan Jones 6. True 7. None 8. Jerry Rice 9. Blue 10. True 11. Houston Oilers 12. Tom Brady 13. John Stephens 14. Brandin Cooks and Aqib Talib 15. John Hannah 16. Laurence Maroney 17. Winning 18. James Develin 19. c) a tri-cornered hat 20. a) 17.5%

Quiz 32: Pot Luck

1. After winning Super Bowl LIII, Tom Brady overtook which former Patriot to become the player with the most wins, regular and postseason combined, in NFL history?

2. After claiming the AFC East in 2019 the Patriots made it how many successive divisional titles in a row?

3. By the end of the 2021 season Bill Belichick was third on the list of most wins by a head coach in NFL history. Who are first and second on that list?

4. Before Sony Michel in 2018 who was the last Patriots rookie running back to rush for 100 yards in a game?

5. True or false – Former Patriots rusher Sam Cunningham is the brother of the former Eagles, Vikings and Cowboys quarterback Randall Cunningham?

6. True or false – The Patriots have played more postseason games than any other team in NFL history?

7. What color are the numbers on New England's home jersey?

8. 'Relentless: A Memoir' is the title of a book penned by which legendary Patriot?

9. Which team was a 2.5-point favorite at Super Bowl LIII – the Patriots or the Rams?

10. What color jerseys did the Patriots wear in their inaugural season?

11. Which 22-year-old defensive back was the youngest player to appear in Super Bowl LIII?

12. Who is the only quarterback to play for the Patriots whose surname starts with the letter Z?

13. True or false – The Patriots were the favorite in every regular season and playoff game during the 2018 season?

14. Which New England running back enjoyed a career year in 2012, rushing for 1,263 yards and 12 touchdowns?

15. Up to the start of the 2022 season, the Patriots had their best regular season win percentage of 0.889 against which opponent?

16. In which round of the 2009 NFL Draft did the Patriots select Julian Edelman?

17. Patriots defender Devin McCourty played college ball at which school?

18. Qualin is the given first name of which New England defensive star?

19. With which pick in the NFL Draft did the Patriots select Mac Jones? a) 14th b) 15th c) 16th

20. During Super Bowl LIII the Patriots forced the Rams to punt on how many consecutive drives? a) six b) seven c) eight

Quiz 31: Answers

1. Kevin Faulk 2. Drew Bledsoe 3. James White 4. St. Louis Rams 5. John Hannah 6. Rob Gronkowski 7. Troy Brown 8. Randy Moss 9. Bruce Armstrong 10. Danny Amendola 11. Curtis Martin 12. Stanley Morgan 13. Logan Mankins 14. Julian Edelman 15. Benjamin Coates 16. Corey Dillon 17. Steve Grogan 18. Jim Nance 19. b) Pittsburgh 20. a) Irving Fryar

Quiz 33: Dominant Defenders

1. Stephon Gilmore spent the first five seasons of his NFL career with which AFC East rival?

2. Who is the only Patriot pass rusher to have recorded 100 career sacks?

3. Which defensive back holds the team record for the most interception return touchdowns with six?

4. After 12 seasons in New England, Willie McGinest spent the final three seasons of his NFL career with which team?

5. Which legendary Patriots linebacker was the co-winner of the NFL Comeback Player of the Year for 2005?

6. Which defensive back's goal line pick in the closing stages of Super Bowl XLIX helped secure a famous win over Seattle?

7. Who became the first defensive player since 'The Fridge' to score an offensive touchdown in the Super Bowl during the Super Bowl XXXVIII-win over the Panthers?

8. Which first-round draft pick intercepted 36 passes during a 13-year career in New England that ran from 1977 through to 1989?

9. Which defender's 18 picks between 2013 and 2018 included six that took place in the final two minutes of the fourth quarter of a game?

10. Which Patriot topped a poll in Sports Illustrated in 2004 where players voted for the dirtiest player in the NFL?

11. True or false – Star linebacker Kyle Van Noy was born in The Netherlands?

12. Who was the only Patriots defender to play in both Super Bowl XXXIX and Super Bowl XLIX?

13. Which linebacker's 24 interceptions in the 1960s are the most by a Patriot who is not a defensive back?

14. In between two spells with the Patriots, defensive back Patrick Chung spent two seasons with which team?

15. Before Trey Flowers in 2016, 2017 and 2018 who was the last Patriot to lead the team in sacks for three straight seasons?

16. Who holds the record for the most career tackles in the Super Bowl?

17. Which defensive star, who joined the Patriots in 2009, retired after Super Bowl LI following a career that included 46 sacks and 5 picks?

18. Who holds the franchise record for the most tackles in playoff games?

19. Which of the following Patriots recorded the most interceptions while with New England? a) Brandon Meriweather b) Logan Ryan c) Asante Samuel

20. Which of the following players recorded the most sacks while with the Patriots? a) Chandler Jones b) Richard Seymour c) Mike Vrabel

Quiz 32: Answers

1. Adam Vinatieri 2. Eleven 3. Don Shula and George Halas 4. Brandon Bolden 5. True 6. False 7. White with red piping 8. Julian Edelman 9. Patriots 10. Red 11. Keion Crossen 12. Scott Zolak 13. False 14. Stevan Ridley 15. Jacksonville 16. Seventh 17. Rutgers 18. Dont'a Hightower 19. b) 15th 20. c) Eight

Quiz 34: Pot Luck

1. The Patriots set the record for the fewest points by a Super Bowl-winning team in Super Bowl LIII. What was the previous record low for a victorious team?

2. Which team set the record with that low score?

3. Before Sony Michel in the 2018 postseason who was the last Patriots back to rush for 100 yards in back-to-back playoff games?

4. Of NFL head coaches with 10 or more postseason games who is the only one with a better playoff winning percentage than Bill Belichick?

5. Which former New England punter threw two touchdown passes for the Jets in a 1999 game against the Patriots?

6. What is the name of Matthew Slater's father who was inducted into the Pro Football Hall of Fame in 2001?

7. Tom Brady holds the NFL record for the most postseason wins by a starting quarterback. Who is second on that list?

8. Whose 15 catches against the Chargers in the 2018 Divisional Round playoff tied the record for the most catches in a postseason game?

9. What color was the color rush uniform worn by the Patriots in 2021?

10. Which Hall of Famer is the only running back with more touchdowns in a single postseason than Sony Michel managed in the 2018 playoffs?

11. Which Patriot defender blocked both a punt and a field goal in a 2010 game against Miami?

12. True or False – The Patriots have never lost a playoff game when they've had the lead at half time?

13. What is the name of the rock song which the Patriots run out to at home games?

14. Which English singer performs that song?

15. Who is the only Patriot to have two punt returns of 60 yards or more in the same game?

16. Who holds the franchise record for the most career receptions by a Patriots running back?

17. Who was the only member of the Patriots' Super Bowl LIII-winning roster that had previously won the Super Bowl with another team?

18. In 2021, the Patriots used their first two Draft picks to select players from which college?

19. If you add up all the points scored by the Patriots in their first six Super Bowl wins what is the total? a) 151 b) 152 c) 153

20. Mac in the name Mac Jones comes from the quarterback's given middle name which is? a) McCardle b) McCorkle c) McKenzie

Quiz 33: Answers

1. Buffalo 2. Andre Tippett 3. Ty Law 4. Cleveland 5. Tedy Bruschi 6. Malcolm Butler 7. Mike Vrabel 8. Raymond Clayborn 9. Duron Harmon 10. Rodney Harrison 11. False 12. Vince Wilfork 13. Nick Buoniconti 14. Philadelphia 15. Brent Williams 16. Rodney Harrison 17. Rob Ninkovich 18. Tedy Bruschi 19. c) Asante Samuel 20. c) Mike Vrabel

Quiz 35: Quarterbacks

1. Who are the two New England quarterbacks to throw for over 4,000 yards in a single season?

2. Tom Brady holds the record for throwing the most touchdown passes in team history. Who is second on that list?

3. The Patriots traded Jimmy Garoppolo to which team?

4. Which backup quarterback had a 10-5 starting record with the Patriots in 2008?

5. Who was the backup quarterback on the 2018 World Championship-winning team?

6. Which quarterback is fourth on the list for the most rushing touchdowns in franchise history?

7. In 2017 the Patriots traded Jacoby Brissett to which team?

8. Which quarterback was drafted by the Patriots, traded to the 49ers and later won two Super Bowls with the Raiders?

9. In January 2021, Pittsburgh's Ben Roethlisberger set the record for the most pass completions in a single NFL game. Which Patriot was the former holder of that record?

10. How many completions did the Patriots QB make to set that record?

11. Which quarterback was the only active player in Super Bowl LI who didn't get into the game?

12. Which former Patriots quarterback gave his name to a video game called 'Maximum Football'?

13. True or false – Drew Bledsoe was selected by the New York Mets in the Major League Baseball Draft?

14. Which popular Patriots quarterback won a ring as Joe Namath's backup in Super Bowl III?

15. Tom Brady holds the team record for the most postseason touchdown passes. Who comes next on that list?

16. Excluding Tom Brady, who was the last Patriots quarterback to throw 20 touchdowns in a single season?

17. Who holds the record for throwing the most interceptions in team history?

18. Who was the last New England quarterback to throw 20 interceptions in a single season?

19. Between September 2010 and September 2013 Tom Brady threw a touchdown pass in how many straight games? a) 51 b) 52 c) 53

20. Drew Bledsoe holds the team record for the most pass attempts in a season with how many? a) 671 b) 681 c) 691

Quiz 34: Answers

1. 14 points 2. Miami 3. Laurence Maroney 4. Vince Lombardi 5. Tom Tupa 6. Jackie Slater 7. Joe Montana 8. James White 9. Navy blue 10. Terrell Davis 11. Patrick Chung 12. False 13. Crazy Train 14. Ozzy Osbourne 15. Gunner Olszewski 16. Kevin Faulk 17. Albert McClellan 18. Alabama 19. a) 151 20. b) McCorkle

Quiz 36: Pot Luck

1. New England's sixth Super Bowl win put them level with which franchise?

2. Which three Patriots had over 100 receiving yards in Super Bowl LII but still ended up on the losing team?

3. Who holds the record for the most Pro Bowl appearances by a Patriots special teamer?

4. Which former Patriots quarterback finished in fifth place in the 2016 edition of the TV talent show 'Dancing With The Stars'?

5. True or false – In their epic 2018 regular season win over the Chiefs New England became the first team in NFL history to go through an entire game without punting or giving up a penalty?

6. Which three-time Super Bowl-winning Patriots defensive lineman later enjoyed a successful career as a professional poker player?

7. True or false – The Patriots were the first franchise in the NFL to buy their own private plane to fly the team to road games?

8. Which two Patriots share the record for the most career punt returns in the Super Bowl with eight?

9. Which defensive player joined the Patriots following a trade with the Eagles in Feb 2019 but was traded to the Cowboys in October of that same year?

10. Which defensive star did the Patriots select with the 21st pick of the 2004 NFL Draft?

11. How many times did the Patriots force the Eagles to punt in Super Bowl LII?

12. True or false – Head coach Bill Belichick was double the age of his opposite number at Super Bowl LIII?

13. Which QB and WR duo were known collectively as the 'Grand Opera'?

14. Who is the only Patriot to have returned at least 20 kickoffs in a season to average over 30 yards per return?

15. Which offensive lineman on the 2018 roster has a father and grandfather who also played in the NFL?

16. Whose 17 forced fumbles between 1996 and 2008 are the most in team history?

17. What number jersey did running back James White wear?

18. If you made a list of the surnames of all the players who appeared in the 2018 World Championship season whose name would be first?

19. How many different players appeared for the Patriots during the whole of the 2018 season? a) 62 b) 63 c) 64

20. Which Patriots star was given the honor of waving the green flag at the 2019 Daytona 500 motor race? a) Tom Brady b) Rob Gronkowski c) Julian Edelman

Quiz 35: Answers

1. Tom Brady and Drew Bledsoe 2. Steve Grogan 3. San Francisco 4. Matt Cassel 5. Brian Hoyer 6. Steve Grogan 7. Indianapolis 8. Jim Plunkett 9. Drew Bledsoe 10. 45 completions 11. Jimmy Garoppolo 12. Doug Flutie 13. False 14. Babe Parilli 15. Tony Eason 16. Matt Cassel 17. Steve Grogan 18. Drew Bledsoe 19. b) 52 games 20. c) 691

Quiz 37: Gillette Stadium

1. In what year did the Patriots play their first game at Gillette Stadium?

2. Who holds the record for the most receiving yards in games at Gillette Stadium?

3. The 2014 Patriots recorded the biggest playoff win at Gillette Stadium, defeating which team 45-7?

4. With 1,635 yards who is the leading rusher in games played at Gillette Stadium?

5. True or false – Every Patriots game hosted at Gillette Stadium has sold out? (excluding games restricted by covid)

6. Whose 350 receptions at Gillette Stadium are the most by a Patriots receiver?

7. Who rushed for a playoff record 166 yards and scored four touchdowns in a January 2014 win over the Colts?

8. The Patriots turned a 24-0 half time deficit into a 34-31 overtime win over which AFC rival in November 2013?

9. Whose 16 catches in a 41-38 win over the Chiefs in September 2002 are the most in a regular season game at Gillette Stadium?

10. Only one team has beaten the Patriots at Gillette Stadium in the playoffs more than once. Which team?

11. Whose 192 receiving yards against the Jets in week 11 of the 2009 season are the most by anyone at Gillette Stadium?

12. Tom Brady holds the record for the most touchdown passes thrown at Gillette Stadium. Who is second on that list?

13. Which team has defeated the Patriots the most times at Gillette Stadium?

14. True or false – Up to the close of the 2020 season the Patriots were a combined 27-2 in regular season games at Gillette Stadium against AFC South opponents?

15. In what year did Gillette Stadium change from grass to artificial turf?

16. What is the name of the Major League Soccer team that calls Gillette Stadium home?

17. Which team did the Patriots defeat 30-14 in the first game hosted at Gillette Stadium?

18. What is the only AFC East rival to win a playoff game at Gillette Stadium?

19. Temperatures dropped to a record low of 4 Fahrenheit in a 2003 playoff win over which team? a) Denver b) Indianapolis c) Tennessee

20. Up to the start of the 2021 season how many regular season games had the Patriots lost at Gillette Stadium? a) 26 b) 27 c) 28

Quiz 36: Answers

1. Pittsburgh 2. Danny Amendola, Rob Gronkowski and Chris Hogan 3. Matthew Slater 4. Doug Flutie 5. True 6. Richard Seymour 7. True 8. Troy Brown and Julian Edelman 9. Michael Bennett 10. Vince Wilfork 11. Once 12. True 13. Babe Parilli & Gino Cappelletti 14. Raymond Clayborn 15. Ted Karras 16. Tedy Bruschi 17. #28 18. Dwayne Allen 19. b) 63 20. c) Julian Edelman

Quiz 38: Pot Luck

1. Before the 2016, 2017 and 2018 Patriots what was the last team to reach three straight Super Bowls?

2. Excluding AFC East teams which opponent did Tom Brady defeat the most times?

3. Which Patriots offensive lineman went on to co-found KEEL Vodka after he retired from football?

4. In 1976 which cornerback became the first Patriot to win the AP Defensive Rookie of the Year Award?

5. Which New England receiver is second on the NFL all-time list for most postseason catches?

6. Which NFL great is at the top of that list?

7. Which defensive back scored a touchdown in the 2001 AFC Championship Game following a blocked field goal and a Troy Brown lateral?

8. The Patriots overturned not one but two 14-point deficits before eventually going on to beat which team 35-31 in the 2014 Divisional round playoff?

9. Which speedy wide receiver caught an 80-yard touchdown pass on the opening play of a 1988 game against the Bears?

10. Which quarterback threw that pass?

11. True or false – Former New England receiver Phillip Dorsett is the son of Hall of Fame running back Tony Dorsett?

12. Which former Patriots tight end later became one of the 'Get Up Crew' on Boston radio station Hot 96.9?

13. The hottest game to feature the Patriots was a 2018 road encounter at which AFC team?

14. If you made a list of the surnames of all the players who appeared in the 2018 World Championship season whose name would be last?

15. Stephen Gostkowski is the co-holder of the record for the most successful field goals in the Super Bowl with which kicker?

16. True or false – Since 2000 the Patriots are unbeaten in games where they've had a 100-yard rusher?

17. Which member of the Patriots Hall of Fame was named the team's wide receivers and kick returns coach for the 2021 season?

18. Which defensive back returned a pick 76 yards for a touchdown against the Ravens in December 2013?

19. How many yards did the Patriots defense allow during Super Bowl LIII against the Rams? a) 260 b) 360 c) 460

20. How many touchdowns did New England score during the 2018 regular season? a) 41 b) 51 c) 61

Quiz 37: Answers

1. 2002 2. Rob Gronkowski 3. Indianapolis 4. Corey Dillon 5. True 6. Wes Welker 7. LeGarrette Blount 8. Denver 9. Troy Brown 10. Baltimore Ravens 11. Wes Welker 12. Peyton Manning 13. New York Jets 14. True 15. 2006 16. New England Revolution 17. Pittsburgh 18. New York Jets 19. c) Tennessee 20. a) 26

Quiz 39: Record Breakers

1. In 2018, who set the franchise record for the most receiving yards in a single season by a Patriots running back?

2. The Patriots are second behind which team on the list for the most consecutive .500 or better seasons?

3. How long was Stephen Gostkowski's franchise-record field goal against the Raiders in 2017?

4. That record was set in which city?

5. True or false – Rob Gronkowski holds the NFL record for the most career postseason receiving yards by a tight end?

6. Tom Brady set the record for the most road wins in NFL history in a 2017 game at the Broncos. Whose record did Brady break?

7. Who are the three players to have started 200 or more games for New England?

8. Which Denver back rushed for a record 227 yards at Gillette Stadium in November 2013 but still ended up on the losing team?

9. Which former Patriot holds the NFL record for the most touchdown catches in a single season?

10. How many TDs did he catch to set that record?

11. Excluding kickers, who is New England's all-time leading point scorer?

12. Who is New England's all-time leading rusher in playoff games?

13. Who holds the franchise record for the most passes defended in a single season?

14. The largest victory in franchise history was a 59-0 drubbing of which team in October 2009?

15. Who holds the franchise record for the most receptions in a single season by a Patriots tight end with 96?

16. Who is the only Patriot to score four touchdowns in a single playoff game?

17. Whose 228 rushing yards in 2018 were the most by a Patriots wide receiver in a single season in team history?

18. Who is the only Patriot to have returned a missed field goal for a touchdown?

19. Including playoff games, New England's longest winning streak stretched to how many games? a) 20 b) 21 c) 22

20. Between 2016 and 2017 the Patriots won how road games in a row? a) 14 b) 15 c) 16

Quiz 38: Answers

1. Buffalo 2. Indianapolis 3. Matt Light 4. Michael Haynes 5. Julian Edelman 6. Jerry Rice 7. Antwan Harris 8. Baltimore 9. Irving Fryar 10. Doug Flutie 11. False 12. Jermaine Wiggins 13. Jacksonville 14. Deatrich Wise 15. Adam Vinatieri 16. False 17. Troy Brown 18. Tavon Wilson 19. a) 260 20. b) 51

Quiz 40: Pot Luck

1. Prior to 2020, when was the last time the Patriots failed to record double-digit wins in a single season?

2. Tom Brady tied an NFL record for the most TD passes in a single game after throwing six against which team in January 2012?

3. In the 2017 divisional round playoff against the Titans Bill Belichick set the record for the most playoff games as a head coach. Whose record did he break?

4. The longest drive in team history ran for how many plays?

5. Who is the only Patriot to catch three touchdown passes in a single playoff game?

6. Up to and including Super Bowl LIII, who are the two Patriot defenders to have started five Super Bowls?

7. In December 2018 Tom Brady became the fourth quarterback in NFL history with 70,000 regular season passing yards. Who were the first three to reach that milestone?

8. Who holds the record for the most Pro Bowl appearances by a New England kicker?

9. What is the only team other than the Patriots to have won a Super Bowl while scoring just a single touchdown?

10. Which Jets linebacker delivered the brutal hit that put Drew Bledsoe out of the game and started the Tom Brady era in New England?

11. True or false – Tedy Bruschi never made it to the Pro Bowl?

12. Who was the only Patriots offensive player named on the NFL's All-Decade Team for the 1990s?

13. Which New England defensive back returned a fumble 47 yards for a score in the 1996 AFC Championship win over the Jaguars?

14. True or false – While with the Patriots, Tom Brady appeared in more Super Bowls than in road playoff games?

15. Do the Patriots have a winning or losing record in Sunday Night games?

16. True or false – In 1970 the Patriots played home games at Harvard Stadium?

17. What is the largest winning margin the Patriots have enjoyed in the Super Bowl?

18. Before James Develin in 2017 who was the last New England full back to receive Pro Bowl recognition?

19. What was quarterback Mac Jones' given first name? a) Mark b) McKenzie c) Michael

20. What was the over/under point spread at Super Bowl LIII? a) 53.5 b) 54.5 c) 55.5

Quiz 39: Answers

1. James White 2. Dallas 3. 62 yards 4. Mexico City 5. True 6. Peyton Manning 7. Tom Brady, Bruce Armstrong and Julius Adams 8. Knowshon Moreno 9. Randy Moss 10. 23 TDs 11. Rob Gronkowski 12. Corey Dillon 13. Ty Law 14. Tennessee 15. Ben Coates 16. LeGarrette Blount 17. Cordarrelle Patterson 18. Ron Burton 19. b) 21 games 20. a) 14

Quiz 41: Coaches

1. Before Bill Belichick, who was the last Patriots head coach to be named the AP NFL Coach of the Year?

2. Has Bill Belichick been more successful or unsuccessful when throwing the challenge flag?

3. The Patriots have won the AFC title under the stewardship of which three head coaches?

4. Who was the offensive coordinator on the 2018 World Championship-winning team?

5. Which 2022 New England assistant coach and former coordinator has a degree in aeronautical engineering?

6. Brian Flores departed the Patriots in 2019 to become the head coach of which team?

7. Which former Bucs head coach was named New England's defensive coordinator in February 2019 but resigned a month later?

8. Which Patriots head coach was 32-32 in regular season and 2-2 in playoff games between 1993 and 1996?

9. Bill Belichick holds the record for the most Super Bowl wins as a head coach. Who is second on that list?

10. Bill Belichick is one of two New England head coaches whose first name and surname start with the same letter. Who is the other?

11. Which 2018 AFC head coach had previously served as a receiver and quarterback coach and offensive coordinator in New England?

12. Who is the only Patriots permanent head coach whose full name starts and ends with the same letter?

13. True or false – Former DC Brian Flores is a nephew of former Raiders coach Tom Flores?

14. True or false – Up to the start of the 2022 season, the Patriots were a perfect 13-0 in home games against rookie quarterbacks in the Bill Belichick era?

15. Bill Belichick has won Super Bowl rings with two teams. The Patriots are one, what is the other?

16. Who is the only opposition head coach with a perfect 2-0 record in playoff games against the Bill Belichick Patriots?

17. True or false – The Patriots under Bill Belichick have never been involved in a tie?

18. Excluding Bill Belichick which Patriots head coach has the best win/loss percentage?

19. Which head coach is second on the list of most wins in franchise history? a) Raymond Berry b) Chuck Fairbanks c) Mike Holovak

20. In what year was Bill Belichick born? a) 1948 b) 1952 c) 1956

Quiz 40: Answers

1. Bill Parcells 2. Denver 3. Tom Landry 4. 19 plays 5. Rob Gronkowski 6. Patrick Chung and Devon McCourty 7. Brett Favre, Peyton Manning and Drew Brees 8. Stephen Gostkowski 9. New York Jets 10. Mo Lewis 11. False 12. Ben Coates 13. Otis Smith 14. Amazingly, true 15. Winning 16. True 17. 10 points 18. Sam Cunningham 19. c) Michael 20. c) 55.5

Quiz 42: Pot Luck

1. Who was the leading point scorer at Super Bowl LIII?

2. Who is older – Bill Belichick or Pete Carroll?

3. Which special teams ace was voted to seven straight Pro Bowls between 2011 and 2017?

4. Who holds the team record for the most rushing yards by a Patriots quarterback in a single game in the Bill Belichick era?

5. Do the Patriots have a winning or losing record in overtime games?

6. Prior to Julian Edelman, who was the last wide receiver to be named the Super Bowl MVP?

7. Which defensive star was team captain every year between 2011 and 2020?

8. True or false – The Patriots haven't scored a touchdown in the first quarter of the Super Bowl in the Bill Belichick era?

9. In November 2018 Tom Brady made his 300th appearance for the Patriots in a game against which AFC South team?

10. Which former Patriots defensive great founded a chain of trampoline parks after retiring from football?

11. After leaving the Patriots offensive coordinator Charlie Weis spent eight years as the head coach of which two colleges?

12. Only one quarterback threw more touchdown passes at his home stadium than Tom Brady did at Foxboro. Which quarterback?

13. The Patriots hold the NFL record for the most wins in postseason games. Which team is second on that list?

14. True or false – Of the eight NFL franchises that started life in the AFL the Patriots were the first to reach 500 wins?

15. Prior to their win in the 1985 AFC Championship Game, the Patriots had lost on all 18 of their previous visits to which stadium?

16. 'Never Give Up' was the title of a book written by which tough Patriots defender?

17. What color jackets are awarded to members of the Patriots Hall of Fame?

18. Between 2000 and 2019 how many times did the Patriots fail to make the playoffs?

19. Tom Brady bought his first house from which Patriots great? a) Tedy Bruschi b) Ty Law c) Andre Tippett

20. How many sacks did New England's dominant offensive line give up during the 2018 regular season? a) 21 b) 23 c) 25

Quiz 41: Answers

1. 2000 2. Successful 3. Bill Belichick, Raymond Berry and Bill Parcells 4. Josh McDaniels 5. Matt Patricia 6. Miami 7. Greg Schiano 8. Bill Parcells 9. Chuck Noll 10. Rod Rust 11. Bill O'Brien 12. Ron Meyer 13. False 14. True 15. New York Giants 16. Tom Coughlin 17. True 18. Pete Carroll 19. c) Mike Holovak 20. b) 1952

Quiz 43: Firsts

1. The Patriots claimed their first Lombardi Trophy after defeating which team in Super Bowl XXXVI?

2. Tom Brady recorded his first win as a starter against which team?

3. Who was the first New England kicker to convert a 50-yard field goal in the postseason?

4. The Patriots were beaten by which opponent in their first AFL Championship appearance?

5. Which team did the Patriots face in their first Super Bowl appearance?

6. Who was the first New England pass catcher to top 1,500 receiving yards in a single season?

7. In 1985 the Patriots secured their first NFL playoff win, defeating which team 26-14?

8. Jim Colclough was the first player in franchise history to do what?

9. Who was the first Patriot to score a touchdown in the Super Bowl?

10. In 1980, who became the first New England kicker to convert over 50 extra points in a season?

11. Who kicked the field goal that gave the Patriots their first Super Bowl win?

12. What was special about New England's 10-7 win over Tampa Bay in December 1988?

13. The Patriots defeated which team in their first Super Bowl appearance played outdoors?

14. What did Tom Brady do in an October 2015 win over the Jets that he'd never done before and has never done since?

15. The 2001 Patriots secured their first postseason overtime win in a controversial encounter against which team?

16. Who was the first New England running back to rush for over 1,000 yards in a single season?

17. How many games did the Patriots win in their first season in the AFL?

18. Which running back was the first player selected by the Patriots in the inaugural AFL Draft?

19. Who was the first head coach in franchise history? a) Mike Holovak b) Clive Rush c) Lou Saban

20. Which New England great was the first Patriots player in team history to score a punt return touchdown? a) Troy Brown b) Michael Haynes c) Stanley Morgan

Quiz 42: Answers

1. Stephen Gostkowski 2. Pete Carroll 3. Matthew Slater 4. Cam Newton 5. Losing 6. Santonio Holmes 7. Devin McCourty 8. True 9. Tennessee 10. Ty Law 11. Notre Dame and Kansas 12. Drew Brees 13. Pittsburgh 14. True 15. The Orange Bowl 16. Tedy Bruschi 17. Red 18. Three times 19. b) Ty Law 20. a) 21

Quiz 44: Pot Luck

1. Which running back led the team in touchdown receptions in 2020 despite grabbing just three of them?

2. Which New England offensive lineman was the first player in NFL history to start in the Super Bowl in each of his first three seasons in the league?

3. In 2018, Stephon Gilmore became the fourth New England cornerback to receive First-Team All-Pro honors. Who are the other three?

4. Tom Brady became the NFL's all-time leader in passing yards (regular and postseason) during a 2018 victory over which division rival?

5. Who was the first Patriot to rush for 100 yards in a single game?

6. Defensive star Patrick Chung was born on which Caribbean island?

7. Bill Belichick has one playoff win as head coach of a team other than the Patriots. Which team?

8. Which speedy former Patriot appears on Twitter under the handle @ceeflashpee84?

9. In a 2013 game against Cleveland, who set the franchise record for the most receiving yards by a Patriots running back in a single game after catching 12 passes for 153 yards?

10. True or false – The Patriots have a 100% winning record in playoff games when they have had a 100-yard rusher?

11. Which team did the Patriots face in the playoff game known as 'The Fog Bowl'?

12. After leaving the Patriots, head coach Bill Parcells took over at which team?

13. True or false – The Patriots were 0-10 in their first ten games that went to overtime?

14. Prior to the start of the 2022 season who was the last Patriot to score three receiving touchdowns in the same game?

15. Which kicker's only career pass resulted in a 4-yard touchdown against the Rams in 2004?

16. Who caught that famous pass?

17. True or false – The Patriots have never had a negative points differential during the Bill Belichick era?

18. True or false – Between 2015 and 2020, no running back in the NFL had more receptions than New England's James White?

19. Tom Brady completed how many consecutive passes against the Giants at Super Bowl XLVI? a) 15 b) 16 c) 17

20. Up to and including Super Bowl LIII, how many times have the Patriots played in the big game? a) nine b) 10 c) 11

Quiz 43: Answers

1. St. Louis Rams 2. Indianapolis 3. Stephen Gostkowski 4. San Diego 5. Chicago Bears 6. Wes Welker 7. New York Jets 8. Score a touchdown 9. Irving Fryar 10. John Smith 11. Adam Vinatieri 12. It was their first ever overtime win 13. Philadelphia 14. Lead the team in rushing yards 15. Oakland 16. Jim Nance 17. Five 18. Ron Burton 19. c) Lou Saban 20. b) Michael Haynes

Quiz 45: Nicknames

Match the Patriot with their nickname

1. Hoody
2. Goat
3. Minitron
4. Big Tuna
5. The Law Firm
6. The Freak
7. The Undertaker
8. Gronk
9. Ocho Cinco
10. The Blazin' Haitian
11. Sweet Feet
12. Flash
13. Clock Killin'
14. Iceman
15. Strap
16. Hog
17. The Experiment

A. Sony Michel
B. Randy Moss
C. Rob Gronkowski
D. James White
E. Bill Belichick
F. Sam Cunningham
G. Corey Dillon
H. Malcolm Butler
I. John Hannah
J. Julian Edelman
K. Bill Parcells
L. The Quiet Stom
M. Vincent Brown
N. Tom Brady
O. Josh Gordon
P. Cordarrelle Patterson
Q. Adam Vinatieri

18. The Quiet Storm   R. Chad Johnson

19. Bam   S. Dion Lewis

20. Jitterbug   T. BenJarvus Green-Ellis

Quiz 44: Answers

1. Rex Burkhead 2. Joe Thuney 3. Ty Law, Asante Samuel and Darrelle Revis 4. New York Jets 5. Ron Burton 6. Jamaica 7. Cleveland 8. Cordarrelle Patterson 9. Shane Vereen 10. True 11. Pittsburgh 12. New York Jets 13. True 14. Martellus Bennett 15. Adam Vinatieri 16. Troy Brown 17. False 18. True 19. b) 16 passes 20. c) 11

Quiz 46: Pot Luck

1. Tom Brady is only one of two quarterbacks to throw for over 400 yards in a single Super Bowl. Who is the other?

2. Which defensive star was inducted into the Patriots Hall of Fame in 2021?

3. In what year did the team change its name from the Boston to New England Patriots?

4. Which former New England defensive star has made cameo appearances in the TV dramas 'Scorpion' and 'S.W.A.T'?

5. Which team has defeated the Patriots the most times in postseason action?

6. True or false – The Patriots hold the NFL record for the most consecutive seasons with at least one playoff win?

7. Which New England rusher was named the AP Offensive Rookie of the Year for 1991?

8. The Rams' Jonny Hecker set the record for the longest punt in Super Bowl history at Super Bowl LIII. Which Patriot previously held that record?

9. Former Patriots quarterback Cam Newton won the NFL MVP Award in 2015 with which team?

10. Who holds the team record for the most career sacks by a Patriots defensive back?

11. Which defensive back, who later enjoyed a successful spell with the Patriots, once ill-advisedly described Randy Moss as a 'slouch'?

12. Who is the lead commentator on New England radio broadcasts?

13. Which former Patriots quarterback is the color analyst?

14. True or false – Wide receiver Julian Edelman played against Rams head coach Sean McVay while at college?

15. Which running back rushed for three touchdowns on his Patriots debut in the 2017 season opener against the Chiefs?

16. Who was the only linebacker to start every game during the 2018 World Championship season?

17. Which former New England tight end is the author of a series of children's books including 'Hey A.J., It's Saturday'?

18. Which two defensive backs were captains on the 2018 World Championship-winning team?

19. Why is Phil Bissell an important figure in Patriots history? a) He threw the team's first touchdown pass b) He kicked the team's first points c) He drew the Pat Patriot logo

20. What is the highest number of takeaways the Patriots have registered in a single season? a) 45 b) 50 c) 55

Quiz 45: Answers

1. Bill Belichick 2. Tom Brady 3. Julian Edelman 4. Bill Parcells 5. BenJarvus Green-Ellis 6. Randy Moss 7. Vincent Brown 8. Rob Gronkowski 9. Chad Johnson 10. Sony Michel 11. James White 12. Josh Gordon 13. Corey Dillon 14. Adam Vinatieri 15. Malcolm Butler 16. John Hannah 17. Cordarrelle Patterson 18. Trey Flowers 19. Sam Cunningham 20. Dion Lewis

Quiz 47: Numbers Game

What number jersey did the players listed below wear?

1. Devin McCourty and Antowain Smith

2. Stephon Gilmore and Darrelle Revis

3. Rob Gronkowski and David Givens

4. Doug Flutie and Brian Hoyer

5. Cordarrelle Patterson and Ben Watson

6. Eugene Wilson and Sony Michel

7. Deion Branch and Wes Welker

8. Babe Parilli and Chris Hogan

9. Ryan Allen and Chris Hanson

10. Tebucky Jones and Rex Burkhead

11. Kyle Van Noy and Chris Slade

12. Kevin Faulk and Jeremy Hill

13. Lawyer Milloy and James Sanders

14. Richard Seymour and Lawrence Guy

15. Joe Thuney and Ryan Wendell

16. Nick Buoniconti and Brandon Lloyd

17. Brandon LaFell and Tom Tupa

18. Patrick Chung and Ron Hall

19. Matthew Slater and Randy Vataha

20. Trey Flowers and Brandon Mitchell

Quiz 46: Answers

1. Kurt Warner 2. Richard Seymour 3. 1971 4. Willie McGinest 5. Denver 6. True 7. Leonard Russell 8. Ryan Allen 9. Carolina 10. Rodney Harrison 11. Darrelle Revis 12. Bob Socci 13. Scott Zolak 14. True 15. Mike Gillislee 16. Kyle Van Noy 17. Martellus Bennett 18. Patrick Chung and Devin McCourty 19. c) He drew the Pat Patriot logo 20. b) 50

Quiz 48: Pot Luck

1. Who holds the record for the most 100-yard receiving games in the playoffs in franchise history?

2. Who holds the franchise record for the most receptions in postseason games?

3. Which offensive lineman was a team captain on the 2018 World Championship team?

4. The Patriots face which opponent on their longest NFL road trip (excluding overseas games)?

5. The Patriots are tied with which AFC rival for the most Super Bowl losses with five?

6. Butch Songin was the first Patriots player to do what?

7. Up to the start of the 2002 season which two NFC teams have the Patriots defeated the most times in franchise history?

8. Who was inducted into the Pro Football Hall of Fame in 1973 and was later named New England's head coach in 1984?

9. True or false – Tom Brady has over 1,000 career rushing yards?

10. Which three Patriots receivers caught passes of 50 yards or more during the 2018 season?

11. Mac Jones threw his first career regular season touchdown pass to which receiver?

12. Which Patriots quarterback boomed a punt 57 yards in a 2008 game against the Bills?

13. Which Miami running back scored a record four rushing touchdowns in a 2008 game against the Patriots?

14. Who is the only New England kicker to convert six field goals in the same game?

15. Which defensive back picked off three passes in a 2009 game against the Jets returning one for a 56-yard touchdown?

16. Who was the unfortunate Jets rookie quarterback who threw the hat-trick of interceptions?

17. Is Tom Brady's career long rush higher or lower than 20 yards?

18. Which future Patriot great's yearbook quote read, "If you want to play with the big boys, you've got to learn to play in the tall grass."

19. What is Ty Law's first name? a) Tajuan b) Tyrell c) Tyrone

20. How are Devin and Jason McCourty related? a) brothers b) cousins c) uncle and nephew

Quiz 47: Answers

1. #32 2. #24 3. #87 4. #2 5. #84 6. #26 7. #83 8. #15 9. #6 10. #34 11. #53 12. #33 13. #36 14. #93 15. #62 16. #84 17. #19 18. #23 19. #18 20. #98

Quiz 49: Anagrams

Re-arrange the letters to make the name of a current or former Patriot.

1. Chile My Son

2. Lowest Fryer

3. High Acorns

4. Ms Even Jailed

5. Mud Ivy Concert

6. Wealth Matters

7. I Invite Armada

8. Tight Malt

9. Yard Bomb

10. Workbook Rings

11. Lanky Envoy

12. Charting Puck

13. A Roller Sport Cantered

14. Ocean Best

15. Dim Your Archers

16. Jute Honey

17. Chosen Jam Lids

18. Joy Roamed

19. Wryly Email Lo

20. Civil New Fork

Quiz 48: Answers

1. Julian Edelman 2. Julian Edelman 3. David Andrews 4. San Francisco 5. Denver 6. Throw a touchdown pass 7. Chicago and New Orleans 8. Raymond Berry 9. True 10. Chris Hogan, Cordarrelle Patterson and Josh Gordon 11. Nelson Agholor 12. Matt Cassel 13. Ronnie Brown 14. Gino Cappelletti 15. Leigh Bodden 16. Mark Sanchez 17. Higher – It's 22 yards 18. Tom Brady 19. a) Tajuan 20. a) Brothers

Quiz 50: Pot Luck

1. Tom Brady holds the NFL record for the most starts by a quarterback in postseason games. Who is second on that list?

2. In 2018, which defensive lineman became the first Patriot since Chandler Jones to record sacks in his first two NFL appearances?

3. Only one AFC team has enjoyed more winning seasons since 1970 than the Patriots. Which one?

4. How many times did Tom Brady throw 35 or more touchdown passes in a regular season for the Patriots?

5. The 2021 Patriots suffered a 47-17 Wild Card loss to which opponent?

6. The Patriots logo is known informally as 'Flying...'?

7. In what year did the Patriots play their first professional game?

8. True or false – The Patriots have lost the coin toss 10 out of 11 times at the Super Bowl?

9. After leaving the Patriots Drew Bledsoe played for which two teams?

10. Which little used rusher scampered for a 42-yard touchdown to seal victory over the Bengals and secure a playoff berth in December 1985?

11. The Patriots routed which divisional rival 38-3 in the 2018 regular season finale?

12. What number jersey did star full back James Develin wear?

13. True or false – Before starting his pro football career Tom Brady spent summer vacations as an intern with the bank Merrill Lynch?

14. In the 2018 NFL Draft the Patriots took two players from which college in the first round?

15. Both Chase Winovich and Ty Law played college football at which school?

16. Brandon Bolden has had two spells with the Patriots. In between, he spent a season with which team?

17. True or false – In the early 1970s the team almost changed its name to the Bay State Patriots?

18. Which three offensive linemen started every game during the 2018 World Championship season?

19. How many turnovers did the Patriots force during the 2018 regular season? a) 18 b) 23 c) 28

20. How many players on New England's Super Bowl LIII roster were drafted by the Patriots? a) 21 b) 22 c) 23

Quiz 49: Answers

1. Sony Michel 2. Trey Flowers 3. Chris Hogan 4. James Develin 5. Devin McCourty 6. Matthew Slater 7. Adam Vinatieri 8. Matt Light 9. Tom Brady 10. Rob Gronkowski 11. Kyle Van Noy 12. Patrick Chung 13. Cordarrelle Patterson 14. Ben Coates 15. Richard Seymour 16. Joe Thuney 17. Josh McDaniels 18. Jerod Mayo 19. Lawyer Milloy 20. Vince Wilfork

Quiz 51: Pot Luck

1. Which Patriot was named the AP NFL Defensive Player of the Year for 2019?

2. The Patriots scored touchdowns from a punt return and a blocked field goal in a 45-0 rout of which opponent in 2020?

3. Tom Brady threw his final touchdown pass as a Patriot to which receiver?

4. Which special teams ace recorded his third career blocked punt in an October 2019 game against the Giants?

5. Which Patriots defender was given the nickname 'Mr February' by Bill Belichick after game-changing Super Bowl performances?

6. Who led the NFL in takeaways in 2020 after intercepting nine passes and recovering two fumbles?

7. In a November 2019 game against the Eagles, who became just the second New England wide receiver in the Bill Belichick era to throw a touchdown pass?

8. Who rushed for 117 yards on just 9 carries in a September 2020 win over the Raiders?

9. Prior to Cam Newton, who was the last Heisman Trophy winner to play for the Patriots?

10. Who holds the franchise record for scoring the most touchdowns in the Super Bowl?

11. Who were the two New England players to rush for more than 500 yards during the 2020 season?

12. Since the AFL/NFL merger in 1970, who holds the record for the most Pro Bowl appearances by a Patriots defensive lineman?

13. True or false – The Patriots hold the NFL record for the most successive winning seasons?

14. Which player holds the NFL record for being involved in the most career victories, regular season and playoffs combined?

15. Who was the previous holder of that record?

16. True or false – The Patriots have never gone winless during a preseason in the Bill Belichick era?

17. Who set a franchise record in 2007 after registering five strip sacks?

18. The 2014 Patriots set a franchise record after blocking how many field goals?

19. Wide receiver N'Keal Harry was born on which Caribbean Island? a) St. Lucia b) St. Kitts c) St. Vincent

20. In a 1989 game against Pittsburgh, the Patriots set a franchise record after running how many offensive plays? a) 74 b) 84 c) 94

Quiz 50: Answers

1. Peyton Manning 2. Deatrich Wise Jr. 3. Pittsburgh 4. Four times 5. Buffalo 6. Elvis 7. 1960 8. False 9. Buffalo and Dallas 10. Robert Weathers 11. New York Jets 12. #46 13. True 14. Georgia 15. Michigan 16. Miami 17. True 18. David Andrews, Trent Brown and Joe Thuney 19. c) 28 turnovers 20. c) 23

Quiz 52: Pot Luck

1. Who scored his first punt return touchdown in a December 2020 win over the Chargers?

2. Who is the only quarterback in franchise history to have worn the #1 jersey?

3. True or false – Tough tackling Patriots defender Rodney Harrison is the brother of the equally tough tackling Pittsburgh linebacker James Harrison?

4. The Patriots acquired the services of offensive lineman Trent Brown for a second time following a trade with which team?

5. Which Patriots quarterback rushed for 103 yards on just seven carries in an October 1976 game against the Jets?

6. Who are the three Patriots to have appeared in the postseason in 11 straight seasons?

7. Which safety was enshrined in the Patriots Hall of Fame in 2019?

8. Who led the team in touchdown receptions for six straight seasons between 1993 and 1998?

9. Who holds the record for the most First-Team All-Pro selections by a Patriots player?

10. Who recorded a pick in four consecutive games during the 2019 season?

11. Which linebacker returned a fumble a franchise record 69 yards in a New Year's Day 2017 game against Miami?

12. The 2019 Patriots set a franchise record after blocking how many punts?

13. Whose 19 opposition fumble recoveries between 1982 and 1993 are the most in franchise history?

14. Tom Brady holds nine of the top 10 positions on the list of most passing yards in a single season by a Patriots quarterback. Who is the other quarterback to feature on that list?

15. True or false – Patriots punter Jake Bailey qualified as a pilot while at college?

16. Complete the title of the autobiography of a Patriots all-time great. 'It's Good to Be...'

17. 'Green Goblin' is the nickname of which defensive star who joined the Patriots in 2021?

18. Who is the only Patriot to score a hat-trick of touchdowns in a single quarter?

19. What does the J in the name of former Patriots defensive back J.C. Jackson stand for? a) Jerald b) Jeremy c) Jerome

20. Long snapper Joe Cardona graduated from which branch of the military? a) Air Force b) Army c) Naval Academy

Quiz 51: Answers

1. Stephon Gilmore 2. L.A. Chargers 3. James White 4. Brandon Bolden 5. Dont'a Hightower 6. J.C. Jackson 7. Julian Edelman 8. Sony Michel 9. Vinny Testaverde 10. Rob Gronkowski 11. Cam Newton and Damien Harris 12. Richard Seymour 13. False 14. Tom Brady 15. Adam Vinatieri 16. False 17. Mike Vrabel 18. Four 19. c) St. Vincent 20. c) 94

Quiz 53: Pot Luck

1. Quarterback Mac Jones played college football at which school?

2. In 2019, the Patriots set an NFL record after recording their 17th straight season with 10 or more wins. Which team was the previous holder of that record?

3. Who was the only Patriots defender to receive Pro Bowl recognition following the 2020 season?

4. Frank Pitts, who was a member of the Chiefs team that won Super Bowl IV, is the grandfather of which Patriots offensive star?

5. Before joining the Patriots, tight end Hunter Henry spent five seasons with which AFC rival?

6. Which New England defensive star is one of only two players to have won multiple college National Championships and Super Bowl titles?

7. Which former Dallas Cowboy is the only other player to have managed that feat?

8. Which defender scored his second career interception return touchdown in a September 2020 game at Seattle?

9. Who holds the record for the most career receiving yards in postseason games by a New England receiver?

10. Which running back rushed for 100 yards on just six carries in a September 1983 game against the Colts?

11. Before Cam Newton in 2020, who was the last Patriots quarterback to catch multiple passes in a single season?

12. Which offensive lineman from the 1970s was enshrined in the Patriots Hall of Fame in 2019?

13. Which player, who spent six seasons in New England, is the only defensive back the history of the NFL with 30 sacks and 30 interceptions?

14. The Patriots hold the NFL record for the most victories in a single decade with 125. Which team was the previous holder of that record?

15. Who led the team in receptions in 2020 but didn't register a single touchdown catch?

16. Other than Stephen Gostkowski, who is the other pure kicker from the Patriots to lead the NFL is scoring?

17. In 2020, the Patriots traded Rob Gronkowski to which team?

18. Lasting 9 minutes 39 seconds, the longest touchdown drive of the Belichick era was orchestrated by which quarterback?

19. Who holds the franchise record for the most receptions in a single season by a Patriots running back? a) Kevin Faulk b) Shane Vereen c) James White

20. How many passes did he catch to set that record? a) 86 b) 87 c) 88

Quiz 52: Answers

1. Gunner Olszewski 2. Cam Newton 3. False 4. Las Vegas Raiders 5. Steve Grogan 6. Tom Brady, Patrick Chung and Matthew Slater 7. Rodney Harrison 8. Benjamin Coates 9. John Hannah 10. Devin McCourty 11. Shea McClennin 12. Four 13. Andre Tippett 14. Drew Bledsoe 15. True 16. Tedy Bruschi 17. Jalen Mills 18. Randy Moss 19. a) Jerald 20. c) Naval Academy

Quiz 54: Pot Luck

1. Who recorded an interception in five straight games during the 2020 season?

2. The longest fumble return touchdown in franchise history was a 68-yarder by which defensive star against the Bills in October 2004?

3. In 1985, who set the franchise record for the most sacks by a Patriots rookie?

4. Who led the Patriots in rushing touchdowns in 2020 with 12?

5. In 2018, which duo became the first pair of players to be selected by the Patriots in the first round of the NFL Draft to have been college teammates?

6. In 2020, who became the first Patriots wide receiver to throw two touchdown passes in a single season?

7. Up to the start of the 2021 season quarterback Brian Hoyer had started games for how many different NFL teams?

8. True or false – Running back James White is related to former NFL receiver Santana Moss?

9. During the 2021 NFL Draft, the Patriots used both their third and fourth round picks to select players from which school?

10. The Patriots finished third in the AFC East in 2020. When was the last time they finished out of the top two in their division?

11. Who are the two players inducted into the Pro Football Hall of Fame who spent their entire career with the Patriots?

12. Which long-serving Patriot scored his first career touchdown after returning a blocked punt for a score in a 2019 win over the Bills?

13. Which Patriot was the only player to score two interception return touchdowns during the 2019 season?

14. Up to the start of the 2022 season, who was the last Patriot to register double-digit sacks in a single season?

15. Stephen Gostkowski holds the top three positions on the list for the most points scored in a single season. Who comes next with 155 points?

16. True or false – Devin McCourty's given first name is Seamus?

17. In 2020, who became the second New England punter to receive Pro Bowl recognition?

18. Who was the only wide receiver selected by the Patriots in the first round of the NFL Draft during the whole of the 1990s?

19. In 1968, the Patriots played a 'home' game against the Jets in which southern city because of a scheduling conflict at their home stadium? a) Birmingham b) Miami c) Nashville

20. What is the highest number of takeaways the Patriots have registered in a single game? a) 8 b) 9 c) 10

Quiz 53: Answers

1. Alabama 2. San Francisco 3. Stephon Gilmore 4. Brandon Bolden 5. L.A. Chargers 6. Dont'a Hightower 7. Russell Maryland 8. Devin McCourty 9. Julian Edelman 10. Robert Weathers 11. Steve Grogan 12. Leon Gray 13. Rodney Harrison 14. Indianapolis 15. Jakobi Meyers 16. John Smith 17. Tampa Bay 18. Mac Jones 19. James White 20. b) 87

Quiz 55: Pot Luck

1. In 2020, who became the first player in franchise history to enjoy a third spell with the Patriots?

2. Who is the highest drafted offensive player in the Bill Belichick era?

3. Of players with 500 or more catches, which Patriot's average of 19.2 yards per catch is the best in NFL history?

4. Which Patriot tied for the NFL lead in 2019 after intercepting six passes?

5. Which NFL head coach from the 2022 season was selected by the Patriots in the sixth round of the 2003 NFL Draft?

6. Which member of the 2020 Patriots roster is a direct descendent of a passenger from the original voyage of the Mayflower?

7. Who are the four Patriots with a punt return touchdown and a receiving touchdown in the same game?

8. Who holds the franchise record for the most rushing attempts in a single game by a Patriots quarterback?

9. Nobody has spent more consecutive seasons coaching in the NFL as Bill Belichick. Which defensive guru, best known for his time in Pittsburgh, was the former holder of that record?

10. True or false – Former Patriots running back Kevin Faulk is a cousin of Hall of Fame rusher Marshall Faulk?

11. Who holds the team record for the most passing yards by a Patriots quarterback in his rookie season?

12. The 2019 Patriots opened the season with how many straight wins?

13. Whose 50 catches during the 2021 season included a team-best nine touchdown receptions?

14. True or false – The Patriots have never had the number one rated defense in the NFL during Bill Belichick's tenure as head coach?

15. The Patriots won their first Super Bowl in which year of Bill Belichick's reign as New England head coach?

16. In 2010, the Patriots tied a franchise record after scoring how many non-offensive touchdowns?

17. True or false - Former Patriots offensive line coach Cole Popovich is the son of the legendary NBA coach Gregg Popovich?

18. Benjamin Watson started and ended his NFL career with the Patriots. He also played for three other teams in between. Which three?

19. Throughout his Patriots career, Tom Brady threw regular season touchdown passes to how many different receivers? a) 67 b) 77 c) 87

20. Throughout his Patriots career, Tom Brady threw postseason touchdown passes to how many different receivers? a) 26 b) 27 c) 28

Quiz 54: Answers

1. J.C. Jackson 2. Richard Seymour 3. Garin Veris 4. Cam Newton 5. Sony Michel and Isaiah Wynn 6. Jakobi Meyers 7. Seven 8. True 9. Oklahoma 10. 2000 11. John Hannah and Andre Tippett 12. Matthew Slater 13. Stephon Gilmore 14. Matt Judon 15. Gino Cappelletti 16. False 17. Jake Bailey 18. Terry Glenn 19. a) Birmingham 20. c) 10